Presented to

Malcolm Rossine

Presented by

Paul Clotfelter

For

Date

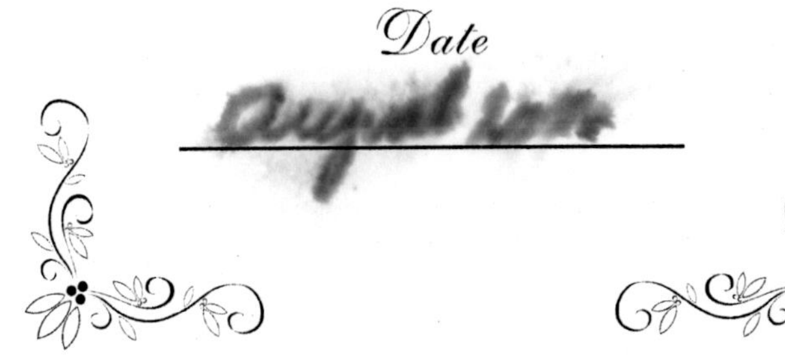

Little Gems of Wisdom: Advice From Grandpa
by J.D. Kroft

Printed in the United States of America
ISBN 1-931232-15-6

All Scripture quotations, unless otherwise indicated, are from the HOLY BIBLE, KING JAMES VERSION.

Xulon* Press
344 Maple Ave. West, #302
Vienna, VA 22180
703-691-7595
XulonPress.com

*An ancient Greek word which means "Book of Life."

Foreword

Every now and then, a special book comes along that seems to fit a niche that others have overlooked. "Little Gems of Wisdom" *appears to be just that.*

J. D. K*roft has collected over many years these hard-to-find epigrams, aphorisms, adages, and proverbs that fall right into certain situations.* Neat*ly alphabetized, these sayings are immediately available to the writer, teacher, or speaker who sometimes feels in desperate need of just the right quote for the occasion.*

Best of all, this is a warmly helpful book for Christians*, selected by a man who has dedicated his life to the kind of testimony that will be upgrading and positive—not only for his own children and grandchildren, but for readers of all ages.*

For *readers interested in a compendium of character-builders (and that should include every parent), this little book will prove to be a very useful and attractive tool.* More *than just a guide for speakers and writers,* "Little Gems of Wisdom" *is a reference source for wholesome living.*

For 1851 *gems like these, the reader has made a very wise purchase and has obtained an excellent bargain in the deal.*

—Dr. D. James Kennedy, PhD
Coral Ridge Ministries

God's book of wisdom, Proverbs, says, "Wisdom is supreme; therefore get wisdom. Though it cost all you have, get understanding" (4:7, NIV). Next to the Bible, these "Little Gems" represent the best collection of wise sayings I have ever seen. I strongly recommend it.

— Dr. Bill Bright, Founder and President,
Campus Crusade for Christ International

"Little Gems of Wisdom: Advice From Grandpa" is a stellar compilation of truth and guidance for the challenges of daily living—an endless reservoir of inspiring thought for all age levels—a vital resource for the public speaker. This book will enhance every library. I know I will refer to it often for my own encouragement.

—Gordon L. Purdy, President (retired)
.Gospel Volunteers at Camp-of-the-Woods

Preface

Perhaps the most meaningful legacy anyone can leave to his heirs, is a set of guidelines for successful living. As a new first-line manager many years ago, I began collecting those adages, quotes, and time-tested truths that I found especially appealing, just for my own edification and use on appropriate occasions. My own interest probably started with those I had learned from my very wise father, such as "He who follows the crowd is always behind", "There is no substitute for work", and "The best way to kill time is to work it to death".

After retiring, I decided to select & compile the best ones for the guidance and benefit of our grandsons: Aaron, Adam, Steven, Todd, and Tom—whose parents (Cherie & Tom, Michael & Kathy, and Kevin & Toni)—have already applied most of them in their own lives. My frequent use of them, in fact, has probably already etched many of them deeply into their brains.

While compiling them, I discovered that most of the ones I was selecting either:

- Strengthen one's character,
- Foster responsible citizenship,
- Enhance spirtual growth, or
- Help calibrate one's moral compass.

I also discovered that such priceless bits of wisdom are not always easy to find—perhaps because they were added to the public domain over many decades, or even centuries, and seem widely scattered into near oblivion among all the anecdotes, stories, poems, and other reference materials that have been exhaustively compiled on a wide variety of topics for use by public speakers.

Although *Little Gems of Wisdom—Advice from Grandpa* is not meant to supplant any of those other collections, if these time-tested truths can benefit either public speakers (or anyone else for that matter) besides my own family, so much the better.

— J. D. Kroft, Author

Pay attention and listen
to the sayings of the wise.

—*Proverbs* 22:17 (NIV)

Acknowledgements

Shortly after I started collecting these adages, I included one of them on the front page of each monthly Newsletter which I edited for the Junior Chamber of Commerce of Endicott, N.Y. A fellow member and lawyer friend, Bob Thomas, mentioned that he always enjoyed seeing those "Little Gems of Wisdom". Since that term stuck in the back of my mind all these years, it seemed like the logical title for this collection. So, thanks Bob, for using that term——which neither of us ever realized would be used as a book title.

I owe a great debt of gratitude to several of my secretaries who dutifully typed these sayings over the years, usually selected the proper category for them, and maintained a file which eventually more than filled a two-inch loose-leaf notebook, plus a thick file folder—- both of which still contain many unused items. As I recall, of all my loyal secretaries, the greatest portion of that task fell on Audrey Dent (now Audrey Baumberger), Julia Powell, Ann Goldman, and Mary Kaminski. To each of them, I say a hearty "Thank You" for a job well done.

I also owe a lot to my sweet, devoted, and wonderful wife, Jean, who not only did a lot of proofreading, but also tolerated the same degree of crankiness (as I culled, re-categorized, sorted, prioritized, and entered these items into my computer in acceptable book form), that I probably exhibit every year when I am wallowing in a sea of Income Tax forms.

But most of the credit for this compilation, of course, goes to the very wise authors of these time-tested truths—-simply for making their wisdom available to all of us.

Give credit where credit is due: Thank God.

—*Our Daily Bread*

About the Compiler

Wisdom is the highest achievement of man.
—Thomas Carlyle

Upon earning his BSEE degree at Purdue University, J. D. Kroft joined IBM. After several early promotions and management assignments which led to his position as Senior Engineer, he served as Advisor to the Director of German Laboratories, and then as a Consultant on IBM's Corporate Staff, which sponsored him as an Alfred P. Sloan Fellow at M.I.T., where he earned his M.S. degree in Industrial Management. He then held numerous management positions in several IBM Divisions, and participated in a variety of cross-industry studies and special task forces. After retiring early from IBM, he served as a consultant for IBM, DuPont, General Telephone, General Radio, and Sealand. He ended his formal career as Vice-President of Quality Assurance for Link Flight Simulation, a Division of the Singer Company.

He has conducted dozens of seminars in five different countries and three universities, has authored several published articles and one other book, and has traveled throughout all 50 states and over 50 countries. He has also been active in numerous community activities including his church, and served as a deacon in one church for 16 years.

J.D. and his wife Jean are the parents of one daughter and two sons who are committed Christians, along with their spouses. It was primarily for the benefit of their five grandsons that he selected these particular quotes, proverbs, and time-tested truths from his files——truths which provide a Guide for Wholesome Living to anyone who wants to benefit from the wisdom of numerous wise and successful people.

Tom Freiling
President/CEO, Xulon Press

It is good to rub and polish your mind against the minds of others.

— Michelle de Montaigne

Table of Contents

Accomplishment 1
Action 1
Advice 4
Age 5
Aim 6
Ambition 9
America 10
Anger 14
Arguments 17
Attitude 18
Authority 20
Beauty 21
Behavior 22
Belief 23
Blessing 25
Boasting 27
Boldness 28
Books 29
Business 30
Capitalism 32
Caution 33
Certainty 33
Challenge 34
Chance 34
Change 35
Character 36
Cheerfulness 39
Children 40
Civilization 43
Common Sense 43

Compassion 45
Compromise 45
Conceit 46
Confidence 48
Conscience 49
Contempt 51
Contentment 52
Conversation 54
Conviction 55
Cooperation 56
Courage 57
Courtesy 58
Criticism 59
Culture 61
Curiosity 62
Cynicism 62
Debts 63
Deeds 64
Democracy 66
Desire 67
Devil 68
Dictators 69
Difficulties 70
Diplomacy 73
Discipline 74
Discretion 75
Doubts 76
Duty 77
Economy 79
Education 80
Efficiency 82
Enemies 83
Energy 84
Enthusiasm 85
Evil 86

Excellence 88
Experience 91
Facts 92
Failure 93
Faith 96
Fame 98
Family 99
Fear 101
Flattery 102
Fools 103
Fortune 105
Friends 106
Future 107
Generosity 108
God 110
Gossip 112
Government 113
Grace 117
Greatness 118
Grief 120
Habit 120
Happiness 122
Hate 127
Health 128
Help 129
History 131
Honesty 132
Honor 134
Hope 135
Humility 136
Ideas 137
Idleness 138
Ignorance 140
Industry 141
Ingenuity 147

Integrity 147
Judgement 149
Justice 150
Kindness 151
Knowledge 153
Laziness 156
Leadership 157
Learning 159
Leisure 162
Liberty 162
Lies 165
Life 166
Light 170
Love 171
Loyalty 173
Luck 174
Man 176
Marriage 178
Maturity 180
Memory 180
Minds 181
Mistakes 184
Money 185
Mothers 187
Motives 188
Opinions 189
Opportunity 191
Patience 194
Peace 196
People 197
Perseverance 198
Perspective 202
Philosophy 205
Pleasure 206
Popularity 207

Poverty 208
Power 208
Praise 210
Prayer 210
Prejudice 213
Pride 213
Principle 216
Progress 216
Purpose 217
Reason 219
Religion 221
Reputation 223
Respect 224
Responsibility 224
Righteousness 226
Risk 227
Sacrifice 228
Safety 229
Salvation 229
Selfishness 230
Silence 231
Sin 232
Speech 233
Spirit 236
Sports 238
Strength 238
Success 239
Talent 243
Taxes 244
Teaching 245
Temperance 247
Temptation 248
Thankfulness 249
Thought 250
Time 252

Tolerance 255
Travel 256
Trust 257
Truth 259
Understanding 263
Value 264
Vanity 265
Victory 266
Virtue 267
Want 269
War 270
Wealth 271
Wisdom 274
Woman 278
World 279
Worry 280

Epilogue 282
Alternate Word Index 284
Postscript 287

ACCOMPLISHMENT

Most folks don't ***accomplish*** more,
simply because they don't ***attempt*** more.

There is ***no*** man who isn't capable of
doing more than he ***thinks*** he can.
—Henry Ford

There are no gains without pains.
—*Benjamin Franklin*

Of a good beginning cometh a good end.
— *John Heywood*

—*Also see Action, Ambition, & Perseverance*

ACTION

Heaven never helps the man who will not act.
—*Sophocles*

The great end of life is not knowledge, but action.
—T.H.*Huxley*

Get action. Sieze the moment.

Man was never intended to be an oyster.
—Theodore Roosevelt

The men who ***do***, are the men who ***know***.
—Marcus Aurelius

Don't only strike while the iron is hot,
but ***make*** it hot by striking.
—Oliver Cromwell

No man knows what he can do best until he exhibits it.
—Ralph Waldo Emerson

To ***be*** nothing is the result of ***doing*** nothing.
—Harry F. Banks

Iron rusts from disuse; water loses its purity from stagnation and in cold weather becomes frozen; even so does ***inaction*** sap the vigors of the mind.
—Leonardo DaVinci

Actions speak louder than words—but not so often.

Action may not always bring happiness;
but there is no happiness without action.
—Benjamin Disraeli

One cannot steer a parked car.

What we think, know, or believe,
matters less than what we ***do***.
—*John Ruskin*

Deeds survive the doers.
—*Horace Mann*

All glory comes from daring to begin.
—*Eugene F. Ware*

Be ye doers of the word, and not hearers only,
deceiving your own selves.
—*James* 1:22

Do what you can, where you are, with what you have.

The man who rows the boat generally
doesn't have time to rock it.

Without **Me,** ye can do nothing.
—*John* 15:5

Nothing is impossible to the man who ***wills***,
and then ***does***; it is the only law of success.
—*Honore Mirabeau*

—*Also see Deeds & Initiative*

ADVICE

He that won't be counselled can't be helped.
—*Benjamin Franklin*

Many receive advice, but only the wise profit from it.
—*Publius Syrus*

To profit from good advice requires
more wisdom than to give it.
—*Churton Collins*

Advice, like water, takes the form
of the vessel it is poured into.

Always take hold of things by the smooth handle.
—*Thomas Jefferson*

How we admire the wisdom of those
who come to us for advice !

Advice is like snow; the softer it falls, the longer
it dwells upon, and the deeper it sinks into the mind.
—*Samuel Taylor Coleridge*

People give advice by the bushel,
but only accept it by the grain.
—*W. R. Alger*

Advice is less necessary to the wise than to fools, but the wise derive the most advantage from it.
—*Francesco Guicciardini*

A good scare is worth more to a man than good advice.
—*Edgar Watson Howe*

—*Also see Knowledge, Learning, and Wisdom.*

AGE

Youth is so sure the rules have changed. Age is sure they haven't. Youth feels it knows how far it can go. Age is deeply aware of the danger. Youth feels it can apply the brakes in time. Age knows it isn't always so.
—*Richard L. Evans*

I am not young enough to know everything.
—*James M. Barrie*

Youth, though it may lack knowledge,
is certainly not devoid of intelligence;
it sees through shams with sharp and terrible eyes.
—*Henry L. Mencken*

Young men have a passion for regarding their elders as senile.

No one grows old by living—
only by losing interest in living.
—*Marie Ray*

Young men ***think*** old men are fools;
but old men ***know*** young men are fools.
—*Chapman*

He who does not honor age, is unworthy of it.

The awesome power of young men
can create ulcers in old men.

Wrinkles should merely
indicate where smiles have been.
—*Mark Twain*

—*Also see* Honor, & Knowledge

AIM

The man who aims at nothing in
particular invariably hits his target.

In the long run, men only hit what they aim at.
—*David Henry Thoreau*

Aim high, but stay on the level.

He who aims at the moon will never hit the mark, but
will surely shoot higher than he who aims at a bush.
—*Philip Sydney*

Always dream & shoot higher than you know you can do.
Don't bother just to be better than your contemporaries
or predecessors. Try to be better than yourself.
—*William Faulkner*

Many are stubborn in pursuit of the path they
have chosen, but few in pursuit of the goal.
—*Friedrich Nietzsche*

Hitch your wagon to a star, keep your seat,
and there you are.
—*Emerson*

Aim above morality. Be not simply good!
Be good ***for*** something.
—*Thoreau*

Once you have missed the first buttonhole,
you'll never manage to button up.
—*Goethe*

You must have long-range goals, to keep from being
frustrated by short-range failures.
—*Charles C. Noble*

To get anywhere, strike out for somewhere,
or you'll get nowhere.
—*Martha Lupton*

When a ship misses its port,
it is seldom the fault of the harbor.

The great thing in this world is not so much where we stand, as in what direction we are moving.
—*Oliver Wendell Holmes*

He that seeks good, procures favor; but he that seeks mischief, it shall surely come to him.
—*Proverbs* 11:27

The main reason men are often useless is because they divide their attention among a multitude of pursuits.
—*Nathaniel Emmons*

The trouble with our age is all signposts,
and no destination.
—*Louis Kronenberger*

Devote earnest effort to planning your life, to setting yourself a goal. Winds and storms will doubtless occasionally force you off course, but surely it is better to have a course to follow than to float rudderless and goalless.
—B.C. *Forbes*

The person who makes a success of living is the one who sees his goal steadily and aims for it unswervingly.
—*Cecil B. De Mille*

Devote your life to something that will last longer than you will.

—*Also see* Motives & Purpose

AMBITION

Things may come to those who wait, but only the things left by those who hustle.
—*Abraham Lincoln*

Lack of willpower and drive cause more failures than lack of intelligence and ability.
—*Harry F. Banks*

Make the most of yourself, for that is all there is to you.
—*Ralph Waldo Emerson*

Better to wear out than rust out.
—*Bishop Cumberland*

Nothing comes; at least nothing good. All has to be fetched.
—*Charles Buxton*

The principle trouble with the easygoing fellow
is that it is so hard to get him started.
—*Bethlehem Pooster*

Initiative is to success what
a lighted match is to a candle.
—O.A.*Battista*

I never did anything worth doing by accident,
nor did any of my inventions come by accident;
they came by work.
—*Thomas Edison*

Be aggressive, but not to the point of being abrasive

—*Also see Accomplishment, Action, & Perseverance*

Ours is the only country deliberately
founded on a good idea.
—*John Gunther*

The strength of our country is the strength
of its religious convictions.
—*Calvin Coolidge*

We should never forget that we created this nation,
not to serve ourselves, but to serve mankind.
—*Woodrow Wilson*

The glory of a nation depends on the
character of its citizens.
—*Herbert Hoover*

Isn't it a striking fact that everybody
in the world looks in our direction?
—*Robert Frost*

The United States is the finest society on a grand
scale that the world has thus far produced.
—*Alfred North Whitehead*

This will remain the land of the free only so long as it
remains the home of the brave.
—*Elmer Davis*

The cause of America is in a great measure the
cause of all mankind. Where, some say, is the king
of America? I'll tell you friend, He reigns above.
—*Thomas Paine*

Whatever America hopes to bring to pass in the world
must first come to pass in the heart of America
.—*Dwight D. Eisenhower*

The foundations of our society and government rest so much on the teachings of the Bible, that it would be difficult to support them, if faith in these teachings should cease to be practically universal in our country.
—*Calvin Coolidge*

Each honest vocation has its own aristocracy, based on excellence of performance. While false snobbery may try to place one vocation above another, you will become a member of the aristocracy in the American sense only by your accomplishments and integrity.
—*James B. Conant*

There may be men who can live without political rights and without opportunity of free individual development, but I think this is intolerable for most Americans.
—*Albert Einstein*

There is a certain blend of courage, integrity, character, and principle which has no satisfactory dictionary name, but has been called different things at different times in different countries. Our American name for it is "guts".

The United States themselves are
essentially the greatest poem.
—*Walt Whitman*

Where liberty dwells, there also is my country.
—*Benjamin Franklin*

Be Americans! Let there be no sectionalism, no North, South, East, or West; you are all dependent on one another and should be in one union. Observe Justice and good faith toward all nations; have neither passionate hatreds nor passionate attachments to any; and be independent politically of all. In one word, be a nation; be Americans, and be true to yourselves.
—*George Washington*

America is the greatest of opportunities, and the worst of influences.
—*George Santayana*

If we win men's hearts throughout the world, it will not be because we are a big country but because we are a great country. Blessing is imposing, but greatness is enduring.
—*Adlai E. Stevenson*

This nation was conceived in liberty and dedicated to the proposition that honest men may disagree. What makes Western civilization worth saving is the freedom of the mind. If we have not the courage to defend that faith, it won't matter whether we are saved or not.
—*Elmer Davis*

I have never had a feeling politically that did not spring from the Declaration of Independence. I have often asked myself what great principle kept this confederacy so long together. It was not merely the separation of the colonies from the motherland, but something in that Declaration giving not only liberty to the people of this country, but hope for the world in the future. This is the sentiment embodied in the Declaration of Independence. I would rather be assassinated on the spot than surrender it.

—*Abraham Lincoln*

In the old days, when the U. S. economy sneezed, the rest of the world caught pneumonia. Now, when our economy sneezes, the rest of the world says "Gesundtheit".

—*Walter H. Heller*

Amazingly, most Americans will defend the Constitution, and yet they've never read it.

—*Also see Democracy & Government*

Anger is only one letter short of danger.

The size of a man can be measured by the size of the
thing that makes him angry.
—J. *Kenfield Morley*

Anger is never without a reason—
but seldom a good one.
—*Benjamin Franklin*

When you are right, you can afford to keep your temper;
when you are wrong you can't afford to lose it.

The worst tempered people I've ever met are
people who knew they were wrong.
—*Wilson Mizner*

Every stroke our fury strikes is sure
to hit ourselves at last.
—*William Penn*

The angriest person in a controversy is the
one most likely to be in the wrong.

An angry man opens his mouth and shuts his eyes.
—*Cato*

Epileptics know by signs when attacks are
imminent and take precautions accordingly;
we must do the same in regard to anger.
—*Seneca*

We must interpret a bad temper as the sign
of an inferiority complex.
—*Alfred Adler*

A wrathful man stirs up strife,
but he who is slow to anger allays contention.
—*Proverbs* 15:18

The one who first gets mad is most always wrong.
—*James Russell Lowell*

A soft answer turns away wrath,
but a harsh word stirs up anger.
—*Proverbs* 15:1

We praise the man who is angry on the right grounds, against the right persons, in the right manner, at the right moment, and for the right length of time.
—*Aristotle*

He who conquers his anger conquers a strong enemy.

He who suppresses a moment's anger,
probably prevents a day of sorrow.
—*Tryon Edwards*

—*Also see Hate*

ARGUMENTS

The best measure of a man's mentality is the importance of the things he will argue about.
—*Margery Wilson*

Behind every argument is someone's ignorance.

We should investigate arguments by the light of the facts.
—*Myson*

Discussion is the exchange of intelligence;
Argument is the exchange if ignorance.
—*Bill Gold*

In a heated argument, we are apt to lose sight of the truth.
—*Publius Syrus*

The more hot arguments you win, the fewer friends you will have.
—*Burton Hillis*

There is no good in arguing with the
inevitable; the only argument available with
an east wind is to put on your overcoat.
—*James Russell Lowell*

—*Also see Conversation & Speech*

ATTITUDE

Success or failure is determined by
attitudes more than by mental capacities.
—*Walter Dill Scott*

The man who thinks he can't is usually right.
—*J.G.Jones*

Nothing can stop the man with the right mental
attitude from achieving his goal; nothing on earth can
help the man with the wrong mental attitude.
—W. W. *Ziege*

Attitudes cannot be dictated;
they must be taught by example.

Our success or our failure is the result of our mental condition—our thoughts about people and about ourselves—our attitudes toward people, and toward ourselves.

—*Dan Custer*

If one goes about thinking that the world is filled with crooks and schemers, then it is. But if one believes it is filled with fine, neighborly, helpful, kindly folks, one finds those people instead.

—*Thomas Dreier*

Shout "you" and whisper "me" and your story will carry straight to the heart of the listener.

Write it on your heart that every day is the best day of the year.

—*Emerson*

We can change our whole life and the attitude of those around us simply by changing ourselves.

—*Rudolph Dreikers*

No life is so hard that you can't make it easier by the way you take it.

—*Ellen Glasgow*

We may not be master of our daily work, but we are
at least master of the spirit in which we do it.
—*Hugh Black*

—*Also see* Failure & Success

AUTHORITY

No man is fit to command another, that
cannot command himself.
—*William Penn*

When the righteous are in authority, the people rejoice;
but when the wicked rule, the people mourn.
—*Proverbs* 29:2

When the people possess no authority,
their rights obtain no respect.
—*George Bancroft*

In any given society, the authority of man over
man runs in inverse proportion to the intellectual development of that society.
—*Pierre Proudhon*

Helping your eldest son pick a college is one of the great educational experiences of life—for the parents. Next to trying to pick his bride, it is the best way to learn that your authority, if not entirely gone, is slipping fast.
—*Sally & James Reston*

—*Also see Dictators, Government, Leadership, & Power*

BEAUTY

Be not dazzled by beauty, but look for those inward qualities which are lasting.
—*Seneca*

That which is beautiful is not always good; but that which is good is always beautiful.
—*Ninon Del'Enclos*

Cheerfulness and contentment are great beautifiers and are famous preservers of youthful looks.
—*Dickens*

Beauty without grace pleases, but does not captivate. It is like bait without a hook.
—*Capiton*

Beauty is worse than wine; it intoxicates both the holder and the beholder.
—*Zimmerman*

Charm is deceitful and beauty is vain, but a woman who fears the Lord shall be praised.
—*Proverbs* 31:30

Beauty may have fair leaves, yet bitter fruit. Beauty without virtue is a curse.

Beautiful young people are accidents of nature, but beautiful old people are works of art.

—*Also see Perspective*

BEHAVIOR

When we are alone, we have our thoughts to watch; in our family, our tempers; and in society, our tongues.
—*Hanna Moore*

To handle yourself, use your head; to handle others, use your heart.

To really know a man, observe his behavior
with a woman, a flat tire, and a child.

Manners require time, as nothing is
more vulgar than haste.
—*Ralph Waldo Emerson*

The sum of behavior is to retain a man's own dignity
without intruding upon the liberty of others.
—*Francis Bacon*

Always put off until tomorrow the things
you should not do today.

Abstain from all appearance of evil.
—I *Thessalonians* 5:22

Always imitate the behavior of the
winners when you lose.
—*George Meredith*

—*Also see Character*

BELIEF

False beliefs and dogmas are the greatest
menace that the human race has to face.
—*Harry Elmer Barnes*

He who does not believe that God is above all, is either a fool or has no experience of life.
—*Caecilius Statius*

If we are to succeed in the great struggle of ideas, we must first of all know ***what*** we believe. We must also become clear in our own minds as to what it is that we want to preserve.
—*Friederich A. Hayek*

Shallow men believe in luck; wise and strong men in cause and effect.
—*Ralph Waldo Emerson*

To believe is to be strong.
Doubt cramps energy. Belief is power.
—*Frederick W. Robertson*

Nothing is so firmly believed as what we least know.
—*Michel de Montaigne*

Men freely believe that which they desire.
—*Julius Caesar*

Nothing is so easy as to deceive oneself, for what we wish, that we readily believe.
—*Demosthenes*

They can conquer who ***believe*** they can.
—*Dryden*

With most people, unbelief in one thing is
founded upon blind belief in another.
—*Georg Lichtenberg*

Man ***is*** what he ***believes***.
—*Anton Chekhov*

A lie always carries a certain amount of
weight with those who ***want*** to believe it.
—E.W. *Rice*

For God so loved the world, that He gave His
one and only Son, that whoever believes in
Him may have eternal life.
—*John* 3:16

If you confess that Jesus Christ is Lord, and
believe in your heart that God raised him
from the dead, you will be saved.
—*Romans* 10:9

—*Also see Faith, Philosophy, Religion. & Salvation*

BLESSING

Sometimes we are so busy adding up our troubles
that we forget to count our blessings.
—*Our Daily Bread*

It is not the thing we ***like*** to do, but liking the thing
we ***have*** to do, that makes life blessed.
—*Goethe*

A thick skin is a gift from God.
—*Konrad Adenauer*

Reflect on your present blessings rather
than your past misfortunes.
—*Dickens*

Sleep, riches, health, and every other
blessing are not truly and fully appreci-
ated until they have been interrupted.
—*Jean Paul Richter*

God provides food for every bird.
But he doesn't deliver it to their nests !!!

He is a man of sense who does not grieve for what he
does not have, but rejoices in what he ***does*** have.
—*Epictetus*

Honor the Lord with thy substance, and with
the first fruits of all thine increase: so shall
thy barns be filled with plenty, and thy
presses shall burst out with new wine.
—*Proverbs* 3: 9 & 10

The gratitude of most men is but a secret
desire of receiving greater benefits.

The well of God's blessings will never run dry.

—*Also see Difficulties & Thankfulness*

BOASTING

He who blows his own horn,
usually plays in a one-man band.

Let another praise you, and not your own mouth;
someone else, and not your own lips.
—*Proverbs* 27:2

The more noise a motor makes, the less
power there is available.
—W.R. McGeary

The more a man boasts, the less self-confidence he has.

—*Also see Conceit, Confidence, Pride, Selfishness, & Vanity*

Boldness

Only the bold get to the top.
—*Publius Syrus*

What you can do, or dream you can do, do it.
Boldness has genius, power, and magic in it.
—*Goethe*

Don't be afraid to take a big step if one is indicated.
You can't cross a chasm in two small jumps.
—*David Lloyd George*

Don't hit at all if it is honorably possible to
avoid hitting; but never hit softly.
—*Theodore Roosevelt*

Put a grain of boldness in everything you do.
—*Baltasar Gracian*

Fortune favors the bold.
—*Cicero*

—*Also see Ambition, Initiative, & Success*

BOOKS

It is chiefly through books that we enjoy
intercourse with superior minds.
—*William E. Channing*

The New Testament is the best book that ever
was, or ever will be, known to the world.
—*Charles Dickens*

Reading is to the mind what exercise is to the body.
—*Steele*

The man who ***does*** not read, has no advantage over the
man who ***cannot*** read. **Both** are illiterate.

Some books are to be tasted, others to be swallowed,
and some few are to be chewed and digested.

There are books of which the backs and
the covers are by far the best parts.
—*Charles Dickens*

The covers of some books are too far apart.
—*Ambrose Bierce*

A man loses contact with reality if he is
not surrounded by his books.
—*Francois Mitterand*

The Bible is a book worth more than all the other books ever printed.

—*Patrick Henry*

—*Also see* Knowledge & Learning

BUSINESS

Business is like riding a bicycle. Either you keep moving or you fall down.

—*John David Wright*

Promptness is the soul of business.

—*Chesterfield*

Not a tenth of us who are in business are doing as well as we could if we merely followed the principles that were known to our grandfathers.

—*William Feather*

Education is to business what fertilizer is to farming.

—W.H. *Pillsbury*

In many businesses, today will end at five o'clock. Those bent on success, however, make today last from yesterday right through tomorrow.

—*Lawrence* H. *Martin*

Doing business without advertising is like
winking at a girl in the dark. You know what
you are doing, but no one else does.
—*Stewart Hederson Britt*

Never shrink from anything your business calls you
to do. The man who is above his business may one
day find his business above him.
—*Daniel Drew*

A business is like an automobile.
It has to be driven to get results.
—B.C.*Forbes*

It is not the crook in modern business that we fear, but
the honest man who doesn't know what he is doing.
—*Owen* D. *Young*

In business, what a man doesn't know, ***does*** hurt him.

Business is like baseball: The hits you made
yesterday won't win the game today.

When you make the job important,
it will return the favor.

Keep thy shop, and thy shop will keep thee.
—*Chapman*

Success in business does not depend upon genius. Any young man of ordinary intelligence who is normally sound and not afraid to work, should succeed in spite of obstacles and handicaps, if he plays the game fairly and keeps everlastingly at it.
—J.C.*Penny*

—*Also see* Education & Success

CAPITALISM

Capitalism is the unequal distribution of blessings. Socialism is the equal distribution of misery.

Capitalism and private ownership are inseparable. Anyone who owns property or has a dollar in his pocket, yet decries the merits of capitalism, is either ignorant or a hypocrite.

The critics of capitalism advocate government ownership of the means of production—the *factories*. But ***factories*** don't produce things. ***People*** produce things. So when the government owns the means of production, it owns the ***people***. But people belong to God, not the government !!

—*Also see Government & Money*

CAUTION

We are confident because of our caution.
—*Epictetus*

The buyer needs a hundred eyes; the seller, but one.
—*Italian Proverb*

Caution is the confidential agent of selfishness
—*Woodrow Wilson*

—*Also see Chance, Luck, Risk, & Discretion*

CERTAINTY

The only certainty is that nothing is certain.
—*Pliny the Elder*

Death and taxes are the only certainties in life, with the latter coming both before and after the former.

We brought nothing into this world, and it is certain we can carry nothing out of it.
—*I Timothy 6:7*

—*Also see Chance & Luck*

CHALLENGE

It is not because things are difficult that we do not dare;
it is because we do not dare, that they are difficult.
—Seneca

Some men rise to the occasion,
while others just go up in the air.

The difficult can be done right away.
The impossible takes a little longer.
—George Santayana

Only he who attempts the absurd is
capable of achieving the impossible.
—Spanish Proverb

—Also see Difficulties

CHANCE

I will study and prepare myself,
and then some day my chance will come.
—Abraham Lincoln

Chance favors the prepared mind.
—Louis Pasteur

Chance fights ever on the side of the prudent.
—Joubert

Any man who has a job has a chance.
—Elbert Hubbard

It ain't enough to get the breaks.
You have to know how to use 'em.
—Huey Long

God Almighty does not throw dice.
—Albert Einstein

—Also see Fear, Luck, Risk, & Safety

CHANGE

The world would be a much better place, if
people lived up to their religious beliefs as
fully as they live up to their incomes.

Self-examination is nearly always the first step
toward change. No one who learns to know himself
remains just what he was before.
—Thomas Mann

The art of progress is to preserve order amid change—
to preserve change amid order.
—*Alfed M. Whitehead*

—*Also see Progress*

CHARACTER

No man can rise above the
limitations of his own character.

The arbiter of everyone's fortune is his own character.
—*Publius Syrus*

Happiness is not the end of life; character is.
—*Henry Ward Beecher*

Society asks of most men more than sheer
intellectual ability. It also demands moral
hardiness, self-discipline, a competitive spirit,
and other qualities that in more old-fash-
ioned terms we might simply call character.
—*Julius Adams Stratton*

One can acquire everything in solitude—
except character.
—*Henri de Stendahl*

Character is no more the fault of your circumstances, than a mirror is responsible for your look.

Character is more easily kept than recovered.
—Thomas Paine

The four cornerstones of character on which this nation was built are: Initiative, Imagination, Individuality, and Independence.
—Captain Eddie Rickenbacker

He who overcomes others is strong, but he who overcomes himself is mightier.
—John H. Patterson

We are more than half what we are by imitation. The great point is to choose good models and to study them with care.
—Lord Chesterfield

A man of intellect is lost unless he unites it to the energy of character.
—Sebastian Chamfort

Character is the total of thousands of small daily strivings to live up to the best that is in us. Character is the final decision to reject whatever is demeaning to oneself or to others, and with confidence and honesty to choose the right.
—Arthur G. Trudeau

Just as a cannon should be one hundred times heavier than the cannon-ball, a man's character should be a hundred times heavier than what he says.

—*David Gregg*

Character and personal force are the only investments that are worth anything.

—*Walt Whitman*

Loud-dressing men and women also have loud characters.

—*Haliburton*

It requires less character to *discover* the faults of others than to *tolerate* them.

—J. *Petit-Senn*

Character is built out of circumstances. From exactly the same materials one man builds palaces, while another builds hovels.

—*George* H. *Lewes*

If you think about what you ought to do for other people, your character will take care of itself. Character is a by-product, and any man who devotes himself to its cultivation in his own case will become a selfish prig.

—*Woodrow Wilson*

Every man is worth just as much as the
things he busies himself with.
—*Marcus Aurelius*

Will is character in action.
—*William McDougall*

Every man must learn to live with the
man he makes of himself.

We are not forced into unpleasant activities. We either
allow them to happen or encourage them to happen.
—*William Saroyan*

It is in trifles, and when he is off his guard,
that a man best shows his character.
—*Arthur Schopenhauer*

—*Also see* Integrity, Maturity, & Virtue

CHEERFULNESS

Those who bring sunshine to the lives of
others cannot keep it from themselves.
—*James M Barrie*

Cheerfulness is the best promoter of health, and as friendly to the mind as to the body.
—*Joseph Addison*

Cheerfulness is health; the opposite, melancholy, is disease.
—*Haliburton*

It is worth a thousand pounds a year to have the habit of looking on the bright side of things.
—*Samuel Johnson*

The true source of cheerfulness is benevolence. The soul that perpetually overflows with kindness and sympathy will always be cheerful.
—*Parke Godwin*

The plainest sign of wisdom is a continual cheerfulness: Her state is like that of things in the regions above the moon—always clear and serene.
—*Michel de Montaigne*

—*Also see Health & Wisdom*

CHILDREN

Children are poor men's riches.

Children need models more than they need critics.
—*Joseph Joubert*

It is easier to build strong children
than it is to repair broken men.
—*Frederick Douglass*

Children may wreck a house, but they make a home.

The best thing you can spend
on your children is your time.
—*Arnold H. Glasgow*

You can do anything with children
if you only play with them.
—*Bismark*

Never say no to a gift from a child.

Upon our children—how they are taught—
rests the fate or fortune of tomorrow's world.
—B.C.*Forbes*

Teach your child to hold his tongue.
He'll learn fast enough to speak.
—*Benjamin Franklin*

A wise son maketh a glad father; but a foolish
son is the heaviness of his mother.
—*Proverbs* 10:1

What greater ornament to a son than a father's glory, or to a father than a son's honorable conduct?
—*Sophocles*

With children use force, with men reason; such is the natural order of things. The wise man requires no law.
—*Jean Jaques Rousseau*

Let thy child's first lesson be obedience,
and the second will be what thou wilt.
—*Benjamin Franklin*

The surest way to make it hard
for children is to make it easy for them.
—*Eleanor Roosevelt*

Train up a child in the way he should go;
and when he is old, he will not depart from it.
—*Proverbs 22:6*

Whatever you would have your children become,
strive to exhibit in your own lives and conversation.
—*Lydia Sigourney*

—*Also see Family & Marriage*

CIVILIZATION

Alcoholism and race consciousness are two conspicuous sources of danger to Western civilization. A mixture of atheism, materialism, socialism, and alcoholism have been the cause of the decline and decay of 19 out of 21 civilizations.

—*Arnold Toynbee*

The true test of any society lies in the character of the people it develops.

—*Emerson*

When in countries that are called civilized, we see age going to the workhouse and youth to the gallows, something must be wrong in the system of government.

—*Thomas Paine*

—*Also see Government*

COMMON SENSE

Common sense is mis-named—
simply because it really isn't very common

Common sense is instinct. Enough of it is genius.

—G.B. *Shaw*

Nothing astonishes men so much as
common sense and plain dealing.
—*Ralph Waldo Emerson*

The average man has five senses: taste, touch,
sight, smell, and hearing. The successful man has
two more: horse and common.

Common sense and good nature will do a lot to make
the pilgrimage of life not too difficult.
—*W. Somerset Maugham*

Common sense is genius dressed in working clothes.
—*Ralph Waldo Emerson*

Common sense is, of all kinds, the most uncommon.
It implies good judgement, sound discretion, and
true and practical wisdom applied to common life.
—*Tryon Edwards*

Horse sense is what keeps a
horse from betting on a man.

—*Also see Discretion, Judgement, & Perspective*

COMPASSION

Sympathy is never wasted until you give it to yourself.
—*John W. Raper*

He who plugs his ears at the cry of the poor,
shall also cry himself—but not be heard.
—*Proverbs* 21:13

To feel much for others, and little for ourselves; to restrain our selfishness, and exercize our benevolent affections, consitutes the perfection of human nature.
—*Adam Smith*

He that despises his neighbor, sins;
but he that has mercy on the poor, is happy.
—*Proverbs* 14:21

—*Also see Generosity & Want*

COMPROMISE

In any compromise between good and evil,
evil always wins.

Compromise makes a good umbrella, but a poor roof.
—*James Russell Lowell*

He who walks in the middle of the
road gets hit from both sides.
—*George P. Schultz*

It is never right to compromise with dishonesty.
—*Henry Cabot Lodge, Jr.*

—*Also see* Diplomacy

CONCEIT

Being wrapped up in yourself
makes a very small package.

Conceit is God's gift to little men.
—*Bruce Barton*

He that falls in love with himself will find no rival.
—*Benjamin Franklin*

The bigger a mans head gets,
the easier it is to fill his shoes.

The certain way to be cheated is to fashion
oneself more cunning than others.
—*Charron*

Half of the harm that is done in this world is due to people who want to feel important. They do not mean to harm. They are absorbed in the endless struggle to think well of themselves.

—T.S. *Elliot*

Good breeding consists of concealing how much we think of ourselves and how little we think of the other person.

—*Mark Twain*

The more you speak of yourself, the more likely you are to lie.

—*Zimmerman*

Conceit is the quicksand of success.

—*Arnold Glasgow*

Conceit causes more conversation than wit.

—*La Rochefoucauld*

If we took away the conceited, there would be more elbowroom in the world.

—*Benjamin Whichcote*

—*Also see Boasting, Pride, Selfishness. & Vanity*

CONFIDENCE

Skill and confidence are an unconquered army.
—*George Herbert*

They are able, because they ***think*** they are able.
—*Virgil*

The rarest personal quality is genuine, deep, sustaining self-confidence. The behavior of the bully, the egotist, the show-off, the whiner, the dictator emanates from a lack of belief in himself
—*Joe Batten*

He who is sure of his motives can advance or retreat with confidence.
—*Goethe*

Have confidence that if you have done a ***little*** thing well, you can do a ***bigger*** thing well also.
—*Storey*

Outstanding work, not boastful conversation, is the expression of self-confidence.

Self-reliance, the height and perfection of man, is reliance on God.
—*Emerson*

He who makes a mouse of himself
will be eaten by the cats.

When a man puts a limit on what he ***will*** do,
he puts a limit on what he ***can*** do.
—*Charles* M. *Schwab*

Confidence is a plant of slow growth in an aged bosom.
—*William* Pitt

Alas, the fearful Unbelief, is unbelief in yourself.
—*Carlyle*

He who does not think too much of himself is
much more esteemed than he imagines.
—*Goethe*

In the fear of the Lord, there is strong confidence.
—*Proverbs* 14:26*a*

—*Also see* Boasting

CONSCIENCE

Conscience is God's built-in warning system
telling you what is right and what is wrong.

Conscience is a man's compass.
—*Vincent VanGogh*

You may not know when you're acting rightly,
but you always know when you are doing wrong.
—*Goethe*

A good conscience is a continual Christmas.
—*Benjamin Franklin*

The world has achieved brilliance without conscience.
Ours is a world of nuclear giants and ethical infants.
—*Gen. Omar Bradley*

If your conscience is your friend,
don't worry about your enemies.

Sometimes, the best tranquilizer is a clear conscience.

Before I can live with other folks, I've got to live
with myself. The one thing that doesn't abide by
majority rule is a person's conscience.

A clean and healthy conscience, a steadfast and
scrupulous integrity—in small things as well as
great—is the most valuable of all possessions, to a
nation as well as to an individual.
—*Henry Van Dyke*

Obedience without the consent of conscience is never a virtue; but disobedience, to be acceptable, must be based on an ethical approach to life.
—Clara Urquart

Never do anything against conscience, even if the state demands it.
—Albert Einstein

He who sacrifices his conscience to ambition, burns a picture to obtain the ashes.
—Chinese Proverb

The only tyrant I accept in this world is the 'still small voice' within me.—Mahatma Ghandi

—Also see Belief

CONTEMPT

No man can fall into contempt but those who deserve it.
—Johnson

—Also see Anger & Hate

CONTENTMENT

The greatest wealth is contentment with a little.

Contentment is the soil in which true joy grows.

Contentment is natural wealth;
luxury is artificial poverty.
—*Socrates*

It is right to be contented with what we have,
but never with what we are.
—*Sir James McIntosh*

The utmost we can hope for in this world is
contentment; if we aim at anything higher, we shall
meet with nothing but grief and disappointment.
—*Joseph Addison*

Contentment makes poor men rich;
discontent makes rich men poor.
—*Benjamin Franklin*

I have learned that in whatsoever state I am,
therewith to be content.
—*Philippians 4:11b*

Let your conversation be without covetousness;
and be content with such things as ye have.
—*Hebrews* 13:5

The secret of contentment is knowing how to
enjoy what you have, and to be able to lose
all desire for things beyond your reach.
—*Lin Yutang*

Contentment doesn't come from doing what
we ***like*** to do, but from liking what we ***must*** do.
—*Wilfred Peterson*

A man cannot be comfortable without his own approval.
—*Mark Twain*

It is necessary to the contentment of
man that he be mentally faithful to himself.
—*Thomas Paine*

Preserve everything in a pure, still heart,
and be thankful for every pulse and every breath.
—*Konrad von Gesner*

When we cannot find contentment in ourselves,
it is useless to seek it elsewhere.
—*La Rochefouclaud*

I am content with what I have, be it little or much.
—*John Bunyan*

From labor, health; from health, contentment springs.
—*James Beattie*

If you have a contented mind, you have
enough to enjoy life with.
—*Plautus*

Content thyself to be obscurely good.
—*Joseph Addison*

—*Also see Happiness & Pleasure*

CONVERSATION

Talking is like playing on the harp; there is as much in laying the hands on the strings to stop their vibrations as there is in twanging them to bring out their music.
—*Oliver Wendell Holmes*

Tears are words that you cannot say.

A word fitly spoken is like apples of
gold in pictures of silver.

Pleasant words are like a honeycomb,
sweetness to the soul, and health to the bones.
—*Proverbs* 16:24

Most of us know ***how*** to say nothing.
Few of us know ***when***.
—*Anonymous*

Conversation may enrich the understanding,
but solitude is the school of genius.
—*Gibson*

Do you see a man hasty in his words?
There is more hope for a fool than for him.
—*Proverbs* 29:20

Think twice before you speak, and then say it to yourself.
—*Elbert Hubbard*

—*Also see Gossip & Speech*

CONVICTION

If you don't know what you ***stand*** for,
you are sure to ***fall*** for something.

Today's mighty oak is just yesterday's nut
that held its ground.

Convictions are the mainsprings of action, the driving
powers of life. What a man lives are his convictions.
—*Francis C. Kelly*

Follow your honest convictions, and be strong.
—*William Thackeray*

Always vote for a principle, even if you vote all alone, and you may cherish the sweet reflection that your vote is never lost.
—*John Quincy Adams*

—*Also see Principles*

COOPERATION

We are born for cooperation, as are the feet, the hands, the eyelids, and the upper and lower jaws.
—*Marcus Aurelius*

Getting along with others is the essence of getting ahead, success being linked with cooperation.
—*Willaim Feather*

Cooperation is not a sentiment—
it is an economic necessity.
—*Charles Steinmetz*

Save possibly in education effects, cooperation can produce no general results that competition will not produce.
—*Henry George*

We would rather have one man or woman
working ***with*** us than working ***for*** us.
—F.W. *Woolworth*

—*Also see Success*

COURAGE

Perfect courage means doing unwitnessed what we
would be capable of doing with the world looking on.
—*La Rochefoucauld*

A man of courage is also full of faith.
—*Cicero*

One man with courage makes a majority.
—*Andrew Jackson*

Fortune never helps the man whose courage fails.
—*Sophocles*

Mental courage is the keynote to success.

The man who lacks courage to make a start
has already reached the finish.
—L.M.*Crandall*

Physical bravery is an animal instinct; moral bravery is a much higher and truer courage.
—*Wendell Phillips*

There is a strength of quiet endurance as significant of courage as the most daring feats of prowess.
—*Henry Tuckerman*

Wait on the Lord. Be of good courage,
and he shall strengthen thy heart.
—*Psalm* 27:14

—*Also see Faith & Success*

COURTESY

Politeness is to human nature what warmth is to wax.
—*Arthur Schopenhauer*

We must be as courteous to a man as
we are to a picture, which we are willing
to give the advantage of good light.
—*Ralph Waldo Emerson*

The small courtesies sweeten life; the great ennoble it.
—*Bovee*

The greater the man, the greater the courtesy.
—*Tennyson*

—*Also see Greatness*

CRITICISM

He who slings mud generally loses ground.
—*Adlai Stevenson*

A mule makes no progress when he's kicking.
Neither does a man.
—E.H. *Cummings*

It is much easier to be critical than to be correct.
—*Benjamin Disraeli*

He has the right to criticize who has the heart to help.
—*Abraham Lincoln*

He who quarrels with the
imperfections of men, censures God.
—*Edmund Burke*

Observe thyself as thy greatest enemy would do;
so shalt thou be thy greatest friend.
—*Jeremy Taylor*

Condemn no poor man, mock no simple man—
which proud fools love to do; but find fault
with yourself and with none other.
—*Roger Ascham*

The trouble with most of us is that we would rather be
ruined by praise than saved by criticism.
—*Norman Vincent Peale*

Great Spirit, grant that I may not criticize my neighbor
until I have walked a mile in his moccasins.
—*Indian Prayer*

The readiest and surest way to get rid of
censure is to correct ourselves
—*Demosthenes*

Sticks and stones are usually thrown
at fruit-bearing trees.
—*W.G. Benham*

A free society is a critical society.
—*John F. Kennedy*

It is ridiculous for any man to criticize the
work of another if he has not distinguished
himself by his own performance.
—*Joseph Addison*

Persecution is the first law of society because it is always easier to suppress criticism than to meet it.
—*Howard Mumford Jones*

They that stand high have many blasts to shake them.

Nothing in life is so exhilarating
as to be shot at without result.
—*Winston Churchill*

—*Also see* Fools

CULTURE

Partial culture runs to the ornate;
extreme culture to simplicity
—*Bovee*

Our culture stems from the knowledge and experience of our forefathers, but we can ***benefit*** from it only by thoroughly studying history, to understand why they made the choices they did.

—*Also see* Man & People

CURIOSITY

Never lose a holy curiosity
—*Albert Einstein*

Curiosity is one characteristic of a vigorous mind.
—*Samuel Johnson*

One of the secrets of life is to keep
our intellectual curiosity acute.
—*William Lyon Phelps*

We should not only ***master*** questions,
but ***act*** upon them.
—*Woodrow Wilson*

—*Also see Ideas, Minds, & Thought*

CYNICISM

It takes a clever man to turn cynic,
and a wise man to be clever enough not to.
—*Fannie Hurst*

Note what people are cynical about, and one can discover what they lack, and subconsciously, beneath their tough condescention, deeply wish they had.
—Harry Emerson Fosdick

Cynics are only happy in making the world as barren to others as they have made it for themselves.
—George Meredith

—Also see Cheerfulness

DEBTS

If a dollar saved is a dollar earned,
then a dollar borrowed is a dollar spent.

He that goes a'borrowing goes a'sorrowing.
—Benjamin Franklin

Debts turn free men into slaves.

You are in danger until you learn
to look upon debts as furies.
—Bulwer-Lytton

A man in debt is so far a slave.
—Ralph Waldo Emerson

Solvency is a matter of temperament, not of income.
—*Logan Pearsall Smith*

Christ paid a debt He didn't owe,
to cancel a debt we couldn't possibly pay.

—*Also see* Economy

DEEDS

Our deeds determine us,
as much as we determine our deeds.
—*George Eliot*

What I ***must*** do is all that concerns me—
not what people think.
—*Emerson*

Keep the faculty of effort alive in you
by a little gratuitous act each day.
—*William James*

He that does good to another,
also does good to himself.
—*Seneca*

Words are cheap and deeds are dear.

Those who bring sunshine to the lives of others
cannot keep it from themselves.
—*James M. Barrie*

Every man is the painter and sculptor of his own life.
—*John Chrystostom*

Let every man prove his own work, and then shall he
have rejoicing in himself alone, and not in another.
—*Galations* 6:4

It costs a man only a little exertion
to bring misfortune on himself.
—*Menander*

That action is best which produces the
greatest happiness for the greatest numbers.
—*Francis Hutcheson*

Even a child is known by his doings, whether
his work be pure, and whether it be right.
—*Proverbs* 20:11

Whatever you do in word or in deed,
do in the name of the Lord Jesus,
giving thanks to God and the Father by Him.
—*Colossians* 3:17

—*Also see Action*

DEMOCRACY

Democracy, believing itself quick with the
seed of religious liberty, laid,
without knowing it, the egg of democracy.
—*James Russell Lowell*

Democracy is a cause that is never won,
but I believe it will never be lost.
—*Charles A. Beard*

Democracy is based upon the conviction that there are
extraordinary possibilities in ordinary people.
—*Harry Emerson Fosdick*

If fifty million people say a foolish thing,
it is still a foolish thing.
—*Anatole France*

The majority can be wrong—and often are.

The vitality and force of leadership in a democracy
spring from the people's making demands upon
that leadership in response to the facts known to
them. Without facts, there are no demands.
Without demands, there is no leadership.
—*Frank Stanton*

—*Also see America & Government*

DESIRE

If a man could have half his wishes
he would double his troubles.
—*Benjamin Franklin*

Man can have only that which he strives for.
—*Arab Proverb*

If you itch for something, you had better
be prepared to scratch for it.

Desire nothing for yourself which you
do not desire for others.
—*Baruch Spinoza*

The easiest thing of all is to deceive oneself;
for what a man wishes he generally believes to be true.
—*Demosthenes*

Set your affection on things above,
not on things on the earth.
—*Colossians* 3:2

To desire to have many books, and never use them,
is like the child that will have a candle burning by
him all the while he is sleeping.
—*Henry Peacham*

To want to be very good, to live at one's
fullest powers, is fundamentally healthy.
—*Marya Mannes*

There is not a person we employ who does not,
like ourselves, desire recognition, praise,
gentleness, forbearance, and patience.
—*Henry Ward Beecher*

Those who dream by day are cognizant of many things
which escape those who dream only by night.
—*Edgar Allen Poe*

Refrain from covetousness, and thy estate shall prosper.
—*Plato*

But he who hates covetousness will prolong his days.
—*Proverbs 28;16b*

—*Also see Contentment*

DEVIL

The devil can cite scripture for his purposes.
—*Shakespeare*

An idle man's brain is the devil's workshop.
—*Bunyan*

The devil loves nothing more than the
intolerance of reformers, and dreads nothing
so much as their charity and patience.
—*J.R. Lowell*

Resist the devil and he will flee from you.
—*James* 4:7

Put on the whole armor of God, that you may
be able to stand against the wiles of the devil.
—*Ephesians* 6:11

—*Also see* Evil & Sin

DICTATORS

Every tyrant who has ever lived, has
believed in freedom—for himself.
—*Elbert Hubbard*

He who tries to control the mind by force is a tyrant,
and he who submits is a slave.
—*Robert G. Ingersoll*

Disregard for human beings is the
first qualification of a dictator.
—*Milton S. Eisenhower*

It is the old practice of despots to use a part of the people to keep the rest in order.

—*Thomas Jefferson*

The time to guard against corruption and tyranny is before they have gotten hold of us. It is better to keep the wolf out of the fold than to trust to drawing his teeth and talons after he shall have entered.

—*Thomas Jefferson.*

Dictators always look good until the last minutes.

—*Thomas G. Masaryk*

—*Also see Authority, Government, Leadership, & Power*

DIFFICULTIES

Difficulties are things that show what men are.

—*Epicurus*

A gem is not polished without rubbing, nor a man made perfect without trials.

—*Chinese Proverb*

The biggest problem in the world could have been solved when it was small.

—*Witter Bynner*

Difficulties strengthen the mind as labor does the body.
—*Seneca*

Splinters on the ladder of life always prick
the hardest when you are sliding down.

Many men owe the grandeur of their lives
to their tremendous difficulties.
—*Charles* H. *Spurgeon*

The difficult can be done right away.
The impossible takes a little longer.
—*George Santayana*

There are two ways of meeting difficulties: you alter the
difficulties, or your alter yourself to meet them.
—*Phyllis Bottome*

The greatest foresight consists in determining
beforehand the time of trouble. For the provident
there are no mischances, and for the careful, no
narrow escapes. We must not put off thought 'til
we are up to the chin in mire. Mature reflection can
get over the most formidable difficulty.
—*Gracian*

The best way out is always through.
—*Robert Frost.*

I've never found a problem that didn't take
longer to correct, than it took to create.
—JDK

Do what we can, summer will have its flies.
—*Ralph Waldo Emerson*

Face up to the situation that there are
no solutions for certain situations.
—*Diana Vreeland*

Every difficulty slurred over will be a
ghost to disturb your repose later.
—*Chopin*

Half the trouble in the world arises from men
trying to anticipate their time and season,
and the other half from trying to prolong them.
—*Arthur Bryant*

Properly defining a problem can be more difficult
than finding a solution. The latter may require
only knowledge or experimentation; but the former
requires intelligence, perception, and sometimes
even considerable experience.

If you come to the end of your rope,
tie a knot and hang on.
—*Douglas Mack*

The wise and active conquer difficulties by
daring to attempt them. Sloth and folly shiver
and shrink at the sight of toil and hazard, and
make the impossibility they fear.
—*Nicholas Rowe*

Misfortunes come in by the door that
has been left open for them.
—*Czech Proverb*

When trouble comes, wise men take to their work;
weak men take to the woods.
—*Elbert Hubbard*

—*Also see Challenge & Wisdom*

DIPLOMACY

Diplomacy is the ability to make a point
without making an enemy.

A gentleman is one who has respect for people
who can be of no possible service to him.
—*Houghton Line*

A diplomat is a man who thinks twice
before saying nothing.
—*Frederick Sawyer*

Molasses catches more flies than vinegar.

—Also see Compromise

DISCIPLINE

You will get much more done if you
crack the whip at ***yourself***.
—Donald Laird

You will never be the person you ***could*** be if pressure,
tension, and discipline are taken away.
—Dr. James G. Bilkey

The most we can get out of life is its discipline for
ourselves, and its usefulness to others.
—Tryton Edwards

Discipline our youth in early life in sound
maxims of moral, political, and religious duties.
—Noah Webster

He that has no government of himself
has no enjoyment of himself.
—Benjamin Whichcote

Life is tons of discipline.
—Robert Frost

He that spares the rod hates his son;
but he that loves him chastens him at times.
—*Proverbs* 13:24

If you discipline your child,
you may deliver his soul from hell.
—*Proverbs* 23:13

—*Also see Character*

DISCRETION

There are two ways to tell whether a cake tastes good. One way is to analyze the recipe and psychoanalyze the cook; the other is to eat the cake.

Great ability without discretion comes
almost invariably to a tragic end.
—*Gambetta*

Discretion in speech is more than eloquence.
—*Bacon*

I know of no safe depository of the ultimate powers
of the society but the people themselves, and if we
think them not enlightened enough to exercize their
control with a wholesome discretion, the remedy is not
to take it from them, but to inform their discretion.
—*Thomas Jefferson*

—*Also see Choice, Judgement, & Perspective*

DOUBTS

Doubt whom you will, but never doubt yourself.
—*Christian Bovee*

He who undervalues himself,
is justly undervalued by others.
—*William Hazlitt*

A person who doubts himself is like a man who
would join his enemies and bear arms against
himself. He makes his failure certain by being the
first person to be convinced of it.
—*Alexander Dumas*

Among the safe courses, the safest of all is to doubt.
—*Spanish Proverb.*

When you doubt, abstain.
—Zoroaster

Give me the benefit of your convictions, if you have any, but keep your doubts to yourself, for I have enough of my own.
—Goethe

Happy are those who have no doubt of themselves.
—Gustave Flaubert

—Also see Confidence & Faith

DUTY

Only aim to do your duty, and mankind will give you credit where you fail.
—Thomas Jefferson

Simple duty hath no place for fear.
—J. G. Whittier

There is little pleasure in the world that is true and sincere, besides the pleasure of doing our duty and doing good.
—John Tillotson

Devotion to duty is a fire that warms us;
but wordly ambition is a fire that consumes us.

To let oneself be bound by a duty from the
moment you see it approaching, is a part of
integrity that alone justifies responsibility.
—*Dag Hammarskjold*

The first qualification of a good manager is his
willingness to accept any duty assigned to him,
within the concepts of good morals and good taste.
The man of unusual capacity is perceptive and
determined to complete tasks beyond the original
assignment, and has faith in people and himself.
—*A.M. Sullivan*

Who escapes a duty, avoids a gain.
—*Theodore Parker*

Duty is what some folks expect from others.
—*Oscar Wilde*

Whenever it is your unquestionable duty
to do a thing, it will benefit you to do it.
—*E.W. Howe*

There's life alone in duty done, and rest alone in striving.
—*John Greeleaf Whittier*

Fear God, and keep his commandments;
for this is the whole duty of man.
—*Ecclesiastes 13:14b*

—*Also see Responsibility & Leadership*

ECONOMY

Take care to be an economist in prosperity;
there is no fear of your being one in adversity.
—*Zimmerman*

The most substantial people are the most frugal, and
make the least show, and live at the least expense.
—*Francis Moore*

Profit is the ignition system of our economic engine.
—*Charles Sawyer*

Economic distress will teach men if anything can,
that realities are less dangerous than fancies, that
factfinding is more effective than faultfinding.
—*Carl Louis Becker.*

Frugality may be termed the daughter of prudence, the
sister of temperance, and the parent of liberty.
—*Samuel Johnson*

The love of economy is the root of all virtue.
—*G.B. Shaw*

The surest way to establish your credit is to work yourself into the position of not needing any.
—*Switzer*

Use it up. Wear it out. Make it do, or do without.

No gain is so certain as that which proceeds from the economical use of that which you already have.
—*Latin Proverb*

—*Also see Prosperity & Wealth*

EDUCATION

Education is to get you to where you can start to learn.
—*George Aiken*

Education is to business what fertilizer is to farming.

Education is useless without the Bible.
—*Noah Webster*

A man's education isn't completed until he dies.
—*Robert E. Lee*

Educated men are as much superior to uneducated men as the living are to the dead.
—*Aristotle*

A man cannot leave a better legacy to the world than a well-educated family.
—*Thomas Scott*

The test and use of man's education is that he finds pleasure in the exercise of his mind.
—*Jacques Barzun*

Too much attention has been paid to making education attractive by smoothing the path as compared with inducing strenuous voluntary effort.
—*Abbot Lowell*

Every person who pursues a career, as distinct from a jobholder, should expect to continue his education for the rest of his professional life.
—*Harry Levinson*

You can lead man to the university, but you can't make him think.
—*Finley Peter Dunne*

The important thing is not so much that every child should be taught, as that every child should be given the wish to learn.
—*John Lubbock*

What is defeat? Nothing but education—
the first step to something better.
—Wendell Phillips

A thorough knowledge of the Bible
is worth more than a college education.
—Theodore Roosevelt

The most successful man in life,
is the man who has the best information.
—Benjamin Disraeli

A man who qualifies himself well for
his calling never fails of employment in it.
—Thomas Jefferson

—Also see Knowledge & Training

EFFICIENCY

The efficient man is the one who
thinks for himself, and thinks long and hard.
—Charles W. Eliot

The average man could probably increase
his efficiency fifty percent.
—Walter Dill Scott

Efficiency without ideals is brutal;
ideals without efficiency are futile.

I don't like a man to be too efficient.
He's likely not to be human enough.-
— *Felix Frankfurter*

—*Also see* Time & Industry

ENEMIES

We make our friends; we make our enemies;
but God makes our next-door neighbor.
—G.K.*Chesterton*

Do good to thy friend to *keep* him;
do good to thy enemy to *gain* him.
—*Benjamin Franklin*

Love your enemies, do good to them that
hate you, bless them that curse you, and pray
for them that despitefully use you.
—*Matthew* 5:44

Pay attention to your enemies, for they
are the first to discover your mistakes.
—*Antisthenes*

Our worst enemies may well be the friends
we once spoke to as only a friend should.

In taking revenge, a man is but equal to his enemy,
but in passing it over, he is superior.
—*Bacon*

Flatterers are the worst kind of enemies
—*Tactitus*

If your enemy is hungry, give him food; if he is thirsty,
give him water; in doing so, you will heap burning coals
on his head, and the Lord will reward you.
—*Proverbs* 25: 21,22

—*Also see* Friends

ENERGY

The world belongs to the energetic
—*Ralph Waldo Emerson*

A man doesn't need brilliance or genius.
All he needs is energy.
—*Albert M. Greenfield*

When a man puts a limit on what he ***will*** do,
he puts a limit on what he ***can*** do.
—*Charles* M. *Schwab*

Men do less than they ought, unless
they do all that they can.
—*Thomas Carlyle*

—*Also see Power & Strength*

ENTHUSIASM

The difference between half a heart and a whole
heart can make the difference between signal
defeat and a splendid victory.
—*Andrew* K. *Boyd*

Enthusiasm is the electric current which
keeps the engine of life going at top speed.
—B.C.*Forbes*

Enthusiasm is the very propeller of progress.
—B.C.*Forbes*

Enthusiasm is at the bottom of all progress. With it
there is accomplishment; without it there are only alibis.
—*Henry Ford*

Nothing great was ever achieved without enthusiasm.
—*Ralph Waldo Emerson*

None are so old as those who have outlived enthusiasm.
—*David Henry Thoreau*

Earnestness is enthusiasm with both feet on the ground.
—*Arnold Glasgow*

Zeal without knowledge is the sister of folly.
—*John Davies*

—*Also see* Progress & Success

EVIL

All that is required for the triumph of evil is that
good men remain silent and do nothing.
—*Edmund Burke*

A thousand people strike at the *branches* of evil,
for everyone who strikes at the *root* of it.
—*Thoreau*

No man is justified in doing evil
on the ground of expediency.
—*Theodore Roosevelt*

Hate what is evil; cling to what is good.
—*Romans* 12:9

Of all the evil spirits, insincerity is the most dangerous.
—*James Froude*

As rust corrupts, so envy corrupts man.
—*Antisthenes*

Men's hearts are not to be set against one another, but set with one another, and all against evil only.
—*Thomas Carlyle*

Enter not into the path of the wicked, and go not in the way of evil men.
—*Proverbs* 4:14

Put on the whole armor of God, that you may be able to stand against the wiles of the devil.
—*Ephesians* 6:11

These six things the Lord hates: yea seven, are an abomination to Him: a proud look, a lying tongue, hands that shed innocent blood, a heart that devises wicked imaginations, feet that are swift in running to mischief, a false witness that speaks lies, and he that sows discord among brethren.
—*Proverbs* 6:16-19

All men's misfortunes proceed from their aversion to being alone; hence gambling, extravagance, dissipation, wine, women, ignorance, slander, envy, and forgetfulness of what we owe to God.
—*Jean de la Bruyere*

The unrighteous shall not inherit the kingdom of God. Be not deceived: neither fornicators, nor idolators, nor adulterers, nor effeminate, nor abusers of themselves with men, nor thieves, nor the coveteous, nor drunkards, nor revilers, nor extortioners, shall inherit the kingdom of God.
—I *Corinthians* 6:9

The highway of the upright is to depart from evil; he who keeps his way preserves his soul.
—*Proverbs* 16:17

—*Also see* Evil & Devil

EXCELLENCE

Well done is better than well said.
—*Benjamin Franklin*

Not 16 % if the human race is engaged in any kind of activity at which they excel.
—*Paul Mairet*

The bitterness of poor quality lingers long after
the sweetness of cheap price is forgotten.

Better to do a little very well, than a lot very poorly.

To reach perfection, we must all pass
through the death of self-effacement.
—*Dag Hammarskjold*

The reward of a thing well done is to have done it.
—*Ralph Waldo Emerson*

Pleasure in the job puts perfection in the work.
—*Aristotle*

Man was created with the desire and the
power for improvement, to which there
is no limit short of perfection.
—*Andrew Carnegie*

A man must give "his best"; and
what a small part of a man "his best" is.
—*Gilbert K. Chesterton*

Achieving excellence is easy—
simply because of all the mediocrity around us.

Not doing more than the average is what
keeps the average down.
—*Wm. M. Winans*

Thinking well is wise; planning well, wiser:
doing well, wisest and best of all.
—*Persian Proverb*

The best preparation for tomorrow is
to do today's work superbly well.
—*Wm. Osler*

Whatever is worth doing at all, is worth doing well.
—*Lord Chesterfield*

If you refuse to accept anything but the best,
you very often get it.
—*Somerset Maugham*

He who does the best that circumstances allow, does
well, and acts nobly; angels could do no more.
—*Edward Young*

Mediocrity obtains more with application,
than superiority without it.
—*Baltasar Gracian*

—*Also see* Integrity & Virtue

EXPERIENCE

Experience is not what happens to you,
it is what you ***do*** with what happens to you.
—*Aldous Huxley*

One thorn of experience is worth a
whole bouquet of warning.
—*Lowell*

Experience is what enables you to recognize
a mistake when you make it again.
—*Earl Wilson*

Experience keeps a dear school,
but fools will learn in no other.
—*Benjamin Franklin*

Fools learn by experience, but the wise by the experience of others; and the way of the guesser is hard.

Experience without learning is better
than learning without experience.
—H.G.*Bohn*

The man who relies solely on experience gets a
very limited education—and expensive too.

A moment of insight is sometimes
worth a lifetime of experience.
—*Oliver Wendell Holmes*

—*Also see Learning*

FACTS

Facts do not cease to exist because they are ignored.
—*Aldous Huxley*

No picture of life can have any veracity
that does not admit the odious facts.
—*Ralph Waldo Emerson*

If you don't look facts in the face,
they have a way of stabbing you in the back.
—*Winston Churchill*

Facts mean nothing unless they are rightly understood,
rightly related, and rightly interpreted.
—R.L.*Long*

Some folks use facts like a drunk uses a lamppost—
to support their position, rather than for illumination.
—*Andrew Lang*

The fact is, nothing comes; at least nothing good.
All good must be fetched.
—*Charles Buxton*

Every fact that is learned becomes a key to other facts.
—E.L. *Youmans*

Facts are like ventriloquists' dummies. Sitting on a wise man's knee they may be made to utter words of wisdom; elsewhere, they say nothing, or talk nonsense, or indulge in sheer diabolism.
—*Aldous Huxley*

—*Also see Truth*

FAILURE

All failure stems from either lack of understanding, or from lack of attention to detail.
There are no other reasons.
—*Dr. Joseph M. Juran*

The difference between failure and success is doing a thing ***nearly*** right and in doing it ***exactly*** right.
—*Edward C. Simmons*

Ninety-nine percent of the failures come from
people who have the habit of making excuses.
—*George Washington Carver*

Defeat isn't bitter if you don't swallow it.

The only bad part of being a good sport
is that you have to lose to prove it.
—*Walter Winchell*

Failures are divided into two classes: those who thought
and never did, and those who did and never thought.
—*John Charles Salak*

It's not a disgrace to fall,
but it ***is*** a disgrace to lie there and grunt.
—*Josh Billings*

In great attempts, it is glorious to even fail.
—*Longinus*

He only is exempt from failures who makes no efforts.
—*Richard Whatley*

A first failure is often a blessing.
—A.L.*Brown*

There are two kinds of failures: the man
who will do nothing he is told, and the
man who will do nothing else.
—*Dr. Perle Thompson*

We learn wisdom from failure much more than from
success. We often discover what ***will*** do, by finding out
what will ***not*** do; and probably he who never made a
mistake never made a discovery.
—*Samuel Smiles*

Failure is more frequently from want
of energy than from want of capital.
—*Daniel Webster.*

The only something you get for nothing is failure.
—*Arnold* H. *Glasgow.*

They never fail who die in a great cause.
—*Lord Byron*

Our greatest glory is not in never falling,
but in rising every time we fall.
—*Confucius*

There is only one real failure possible,
and that is to not be true to the best one knows.

Lack of willpower and drive cause more
failures than lack of intelligence & ability.
—*Harry F. Banks*

When a man no longer wants to improve, he is done for.

Defeat is nothing but the first step to something better.
—*Wendell Phillips*

By failing to prepare, you are preparing to fail.
—*Benjamin Franklin*

A failure is a man who has blundered,
but not been able to cash in on the experience.
—*Elbert Hubbard*

—*Also see Mistakes*

FAITH

Faith is to believe what we do not see;
and the reward of this faith is to see what we believe.
—*St. Augustine*

Faith is knowing there is an ocean
because you have seen a brook.
—*William Arthur Ward*

Straight is the way, and narrow is the gate,
which leads to life, and there are few who find it.
—*Matt.* 7:14

Keep the faith, but not to yourself.

Our faith and our friendships are not shattered
by one big act but by many small neglects.
—*J.Gustav White*

A perfect faith would lift us absolutely above fear.
—*George MacDonald*

I am the way, the truth, and the life.
—*John* 4:6

You can never win a battle without faith in your ability.

Nothing in life is more wonderful than faith—
the one great moving force which we can neither
weigh in the balance nor test in the crucible.
—*William Osler*

Next to faith in God, is faith in labor.
—*Christian Bovee*

After nearly 2 centuries of passionate struggles,
neither science nor faith has succeeded in discrediting
the other. On the contrary, it is obvious that neither can
develop normally without the other—simply because
the same life animates both; neither in its impetus nor
its achievements can science go to its limits without
becoming tinged with mysticism charged with faith.
—*Pierre Teilhard de Chardin*

The just shall live by faith.
—*Romans* 1:17

He who loses money, loses much; he who loses a friend,
loses much more; he who loses faith, loses all.

For as the body without the spirit is dead,
faith without works is dead also.
—*James* 2:26

—*Also see Belief, Philosophy, Religion, & Salvation*

FAME

Fame usually comes to those who
are thinking about something else.
—*Oliver Wendell Holmes*

A man who is contented with what he ***has*** done,
will never be famous for what he ***will*** do.
—*Fred Estabrook*

Fame is a fickle food upon a shifting plate.
—*Emily Dickinson*

Making myself known is not what is uppermost in my mind. I am aiming at something better: to please myself.
—*Gustave Flaubert*

Carve your name on hearts,
instead of on trees or in marble.

—*Also see Greatness & Popularity*

FAMILY

Children need models more than they need critics.
—*Joseph Joubert*

The best legacy a parent can leave his
children is more of his time every day.
—O.A.*Battista*

If you want to be proud of your children, then live
in such a way that they will be proud of you.

The ability to say "No" is perhaps
the greatest gift a parent has.
—*Sam Levinson*

Parenthood is a sacred obligation that bears
compound interest through the years.
—*Arnold Glasgow.*

The family has become too scared of its children; the children too insecure in their remoteness from their parents; and the church too much of a social welfare organization for the good of the family, the church, or society.
—A. *Whitney Griswold*

Where there is room in the heart,
there is always room in the house.
—*Thomas Moore*

A wise son makes a glad father;
but a foolish man despises his mother.
—*Proverbs* 15:20

There is too much stress today on material things. Teach your children not so much the value of cents, but the sense of values.
—*Morris Franklin*

There is no better place to bring up a family than in a rural environment. There's something about getting up at 5 AM, feeding the chickens and livestock, and milking a couple of cows before breakfast that gives you a life-long respect for the price of butter and eggs.
—*William Vaughn*

—*Also see Children & Marriage*

FEAR

A man who's afraid to start is even worse than a quitter.

A superior man is one who
is free from fear and anxieties.
—*Confucious*

Fear is the mother of safety.
—*Burke*

Fear is faithlessness.
—*George MacDonald*

Suspicion always haunts the guilty mind;
The thief doth fear each bush an officer.

We must face what we fear.
—*Max Lerner*

Let the fear of a danger be the spur to prevent it.
—*Quarles*

The only thing we have to fear on this planet is man.
—*Carl Jung*

A man who causes fear cannot be free from fear.
—*Epicurus*

Two fears should follow us through life. There is the fear that we won't prove worthy in the eyes of someone who knows us as well as we know ourselves. That is the fear of God. And there is the fear of Man—the fear that men won't understand us and we shall be cut off from them.
—*Robert Frost*

—*Also see* Faith, Failure, & Risk

FLATTERY

Imitation is the sincerest form of flattery.
—*C. C. Colton*

When a man is really important,
the worst advisor he can have is a flatterer.
—*Gerald W. Johnson*

Flattery is never so agreeable as to our blind side;
commend a fool for his wit, or a knave for his honesty,
and they will receive you into their bosom.
—Henry Fielding

Flattery is the food of fools. Yet, now and then
men of wit will condescend to take a bit.
—Jonathon Swift

A flattering mouth works ruin.
—Proverbs 26:28b

—Also see Speech

FOOLS

Fools despise wisdom and instruction.
—Proverbs 1:7b

Any fool can criticize, condemn,
and complain—and most fools do.
—Dale Carnegie

None but a fool is always right.
—Hare

The biggest fool is the man who fools himself.

The heart of a fool is in his *mouth*,
but the mouth of a wise man is in his *heart*.
—*Benjamin Franklin*

To make a trade of laughing at a fool
is the highway to becoming one.
—*Thomas Fuller*

A fool despises his father's instruction,
but he who receives reproof is prudent.
—*Proverbs* 15:5

Every absurdity has a champion to defend it.
—*Oliver Goldsmith*

The ultimate result of shielding men from the
effects of folly is to fill the world with fools.
—*Herbert Spencer*

An educated fool is more foolish than an ignorant one.
—*Moliere*

Even a fool is counted wise when he holds his peace;
when he shuts his lips, he is considered perceptive.
—*Proverbs* 17:28

The greatest of faults is to be conscious of none.
—*Carlyle*

—*Also see* Wisdom

FORTUNE

When prosperity comes, do not use all of it.

—*Confucius*

Noble blood is an accident of fortune,
noble actions characterize the great.

—*Goldoni*

A great fortune is a great slavery.

—*Seneca*

Not many men have both good fortune and good sense.

—*Livy*

Fortune, when she caresses a man too much,
makes him a fool.

—*Publius Syrus*

Nothing is more perilous to men
than a sudden change of fortune.

—*Quintillian*

Fortune does not change men; it unmasks them.

—*Suzanne Necker*

—*Also see Wealth*

FRIENDS

The only way to make a friend is to be one.
—*Emerson*

Your companions are like an elevator—they will either take you up, or they will take you down.

A friend to everybody is a friend to nobody.
—*Spanish Proverb*

The only truly friendless people are those who are too well off to need help, but too selfish to provide any.
—*Christian Neville Bovee*

The righteous should choose his friends carefully, for the way of the wicked leads them astray.
—*Proverbs* 12:26 (NIV)

He who lies down with dogs,
shall surely rise up with fleas.
—*Benjamin Franklin*

A true friend doesn't sympathize with your weakness—he helps summon your strength.
—*Arnold Glasgow*

If a man does not make new acquaintances as he advances through life he will soon find himself alone. A man should keep his friendship in constant repair.

—*Samuel Johnson*

You will make more friends in a week by getting yourself interested in other people than you can in a year by trying to get other people interested in you.

—*Arnold Bennett*

Make more friends. Almost anyone will make a better friend than an enemy.

—*Emerson*

A friend loves at all times.

—*Proverbs 17:17a*

Many people will walk in and out of your life, but only true friends will leave footprints on your heart.

—*Eleanor Roosevelt*

—*Also see Enemies*

FUTURE

The future is purchased by the present.

—*Samuel Johnson*

No sensible man watches his feet hit the ground. He looks ahead to see what kind of ground they'll hit next.
—*Ernest Haycock*

I like the dreams of the future better than the history of the past.
—*Thomas Jefferson*

Fate leads the willing, and drags along those who hang back.
—*Seneca*

Real generosity toward the future consists in giving our all to what is present.
—*Albert Camus*

—*Also see Common Sense*

GENEROSITY

As the purse is emptied, the heart is filled.
—*Victor Hugo*

The most sensitive part of the human anatomy is the wallet.

If you are not a ***recipient*** of charity, you should be a ***contributor*** to it.

It is better to give than to lend,
and it costs about the same.
—*Sir Philip Gibbs*

It is not what we ***take*** up,
but what we ***give*** up, that makes us rich.
—*Henry Ward Beecher*

He that gives to the poor will not lack; but he
that hides his eyes shall have many a curse.
—*Proverbs* 28:27

We make a living by what we get,
but we make a life by what we give.
—*Norman MacEwan*

Those who give, have all things;
they who withhold, have nothing.
—*Hindu Proverb*

The high-minded man is fond of conferring benefits,
but it shames him to receive them.
—*Aristotle*

He who gives what he would as readily throw
away, gives without generosity; for the
essence of generosity is in self-sacrifice.
—*John Taylor*

The sacrifice of the wicked is detestable—
how much more so, when brought with evil intent.
—*Proverbs* 21:27

It is more blessed to give than to receive.
—*Acts* 20: 35

Many give their lives for their country,
but Jesus gave **His** life for the world !!

—*Also see Sacrifice & Want*

Many people want to serve God
only in an advisory capacity.

Attempt as much ***for*** God as you expect ***from*** God.

God gives, but man must open his hand.
—*German Proverb*

Sometimes God gives you a little,
to see what you'd do with a lot.

God visits us often, but frequently we aren't at home.
—*Joseph Roox*

God is more interested in your availability,
than in your ability.

Man is never higher than when
he is on his knees before God.

My concern is not whether God is on our side,
but whether we are on God's side.
—*Abraham Lincoln*

Nobody talks so constantly about God
as those who say there ***is*** no God.
—*Heywood Brown*

You may be out of God's will,
but you're never out of His reach.

He who does not believe that God is above all,
is either a fool or has no experience of life.
—*Caecilius Statius*

God helps those who help themselves.
—*Benjamin Franklin*

Better the world know you as a sinner,
than for God to know you as a hypocrite.
—*Danish Proverb*

A man with God is always in the majority.
—*John Knox*

A man should hear some music, read some poetry, and see a fine picture every day of his life, so that worldly cares may not obliterate the sense of beauty which God has implanted in the human soul.

—*Goethe*

Cut off from the worship of the divine, liesure becomes laziness and work inhuman.

—*John Piper*

God should never have been expelled from American classrooms in the first place.

—*Ronald Reagan*

There are two things I've learned:
There ***is*** a God. And I'm ***not*** Him.

And God is able to make all grace abound toward you; that ye, always having all sufficiency in all things, may abound to every good work.

—II *Corinthians* 9:8

—*Also see Belief, Faith, Religion, & Salvation*

GOSSIP

A dog has a lot of friends because he wags his tail instead of his tongue.

If you would keep your secret from
an enemy, tell it not to a friend.
—*Benjamin Franklin*

Without wood, a fire goes out;
without gossip, a quarrel dies down.
—*Proverbs* 26:20 (NIV)

A gossip betrays a confidence;
so avoid a man who talks too much.
—*Proverbs* 20:19 (NIV)

A gossip betrays a confidence,
but a trustworthy man keeps a secret.
—*Proverbs* 11:13 (NIV)

All hard work brings a profit,
but mere talk leads only to poverty.
—*Proverbs* 14:23 (NIV)

—*Also see Conversation & Speech*

GOVERNMENT

Government is a dangerous servant,
and a fearful master.
—*George Washington*

Those who will not be governed by
God will be ruled by tyrants.
—*William Penn*

When public service ceases to be the chief
business of the citizens, and they would
rather serve with their money than with their
persons, the state is not far from its fall.
—*Jean-Jacques Rousseau*

The government is **us**; **we** are the
government**—you and I**.
—*Theodore Roosevelt (If we citizens don't participate in
the governing process, as our Constitution specifies,
we will continue to lose our freedoms—one by one.
Our Congressmen are our* EMPLOYEES *—not our Rulers*!!
Shouldn't we therefore be giving them some direction ??)

Let us never forget that the ultimate rulers are not a
President, our Congressmen, Senators, and government
officials, but the voters themselves.
—*Franklin Delano Roosevelt*

**Society is in danger when those who have never
learned to obey, are given the right to command**.
—*Bishop Fulton J. Sheen*

Government can give you ***nothing***
that it doesn't first take away from ***some*****body**.

When a minority becomes a majority
and gains authority, it hates a minority.
—*L.H.Robbins*

The philosophy of the schoolroom in one generation
will be the philosophy of government in the next.
—*Abraham Lincoln*

No matter how noble the objectives of a government, if
it blurs decency and kindness, cheapens human life, and
breeds ill will and suspicion, it is an evil government.
—*Eric Hoffer*

The test of any government is the extent to
which it increases the good in the people.
—*Aristotle*

**When there is a lack of honor in government,
the morals of the whole people are poisoned**.
—*Herbert Hoover*

Bureaucracy, the rule of no one,
has become the modern form of despotism.
—*Mary McCarthy*

Self-government is the ***natural*** government of man.
—*Henry Clay*

The face of tyranny is always mild at first.

Government is not a substitute for people,
but simply the instrument through which they
act. In the last analysis, the only freedom is
the freedom to discipline ourselves.
—*Bernard Baruch*

The office of government is not to confer
happiness, but to give men the opportunity
to work out happiness for themselves.
—*William Ellery Channing*

There is one thing better than good government, and
that is government in which all the people take part.
—*Walter Hines*

We must not confuse patriotism with
blind endorsement of bad policies.
—*Mark O. Hatfield*

Democracy is the worst form of government—
except all others.
—*Winston Churchill*

Without true Christian principles,
conservatism is a political philosophy
of selfishness, and liberalism is one of greed.
—*Thomas C. Jeffrey*

Democracy is based on the conviction that there are extraordinary possibilities in ordinary people.
—*Harry Emerson Fosdick*

It is error alone which needs the support of government; truth can stand by itself.
—*Thomas Jefferson*

—*Also see Authority, Dictators, Leadership, & Power*

GRACE

Your worst days are never so bad that you are beyond the *reach* of God's grace. And your best days are never so good that you are beyond the *need* of God's grace.

By grace, you are saved through faith, and that not of yourselves. It is the gift of God, not of works, lest anyone should boast.
—*Ephesians* 2:8,9

—*Also see Faith, God, & Religion*

GREATNESS

Great minds have purposes; others have wishes.
—*Washington Irving*

If any man seeks greatness, let him forget
greatness and ask for truth, and he shall find both.
—*Horace Mann*

Each man is a hero and an oracle to somebody.
—*Ralph Waldo Emerson*

The price of greatness is responsibility.

The truest mark of having been born with
great qualities, is being born without envy.
—*La Rochefoucald*

When love and skill work together, expect a masterpiece.
—*Ruskin*

It is not sufficient to have great qualities;
we must be able to make proper use of them.
—*La Rochefoucald*

Every great man is always being helped
by everybody; for his gift is to get the
good out of all things and all persons.
—*John Ruskin*

Great men are more distinguished by range
and extent than by originality.
—*Ralph Waldo Emerson*

Those who give too much attention to trifling things,
become generally incapable of great ones.
—*La Rochefoucauld*

The true measure of a man is not in the number of
servants he has, but in the number of people he serves.
—*Arnold Glasgow*

One great lesson learned from the study of lives
of notable men is that patience, perseverance, stick-to-
itiveness and unflagging courage are essential qualities.
—B.C.*Forbes*

It is better to dare mighty things, to win glorious
triumphs, even though checkered by failure, than
to join those who neither enjoy much or suffer
much—because they live in the gray twilight that
know neither victory nor defeat.
—*Theodore Roosevelt*

It doesn't take great men to do things,
but it is doing things that makes men great.
—*Arnold Glasgow*

I have known 95 of the world's great men in my time, and of these 87 were followers of the Bible.
—*William Gladstone*

—*Also see* Fame

Grief

Grief is the agony of an instant,
but to indulge in it is a major blunder.
—*Benjamin Disraeli*

Everyone can master a grief, but he that has it.
—*Shakespeare*

Those who have known grief, seldom seem sad.
—*Disraeli*

—*Also see* Difficulties

Habit

Habit is either the best of servants—
or the worst of masters.
—*Nathaniel Perlman*

The nature of men is always the same.
It is their habits that separate them.
—*Confucious*

A man who is at the top, is a man who has
the habit of getting to the bottom of things.
—*Joseph* E. *Rogers*

Good habits come from resisting temptation.

The measure of our success is usually
the measure of our habits.

It is easy to assume a habit; but when you
try to cast it off, it will take skin and all.
—*Henry Wheeler Shaw*

Habit, if not resisted, soon becomes necessity.
—*St. Augustine*

The chains of habit are generally too small to be felt,
until they are too strong to be broken.
—*Samuel Johnson*

—*Also see Success*

HAPPINESS

Most folks are just about as happy
as they make up their minds to be.
—*Abraham Lincoln*

Success is getting what you want.
Happiness is wanting what you get.
—*Dave Gardner*

Happiness isn't attained through self-gratification,
but through fidelity to a worthy purpose.
—*Helen Keller*

Happiness is a habit. Cultivate it.
—*Elbert Hubbard*

Happy are those people whose God is the Lord.
—*Psalm 144:15b*

If we only wanted to be happy it would be
easy; but we want to be happier than other
people, which is almost always difficult, since
we think them to be happier than they are.
—*Charles de Montesquieu*

Our greatest happiness is always the result of
a good conscience, good health, occupation,
and freedom in all just pursuits.
—*Thomas Jefferson*

To be happy is not the purpose of our being,
but to ***deserve*** happiness.
—*Immanuel Fichte*

Happiness can be found only through
expressing all one's physical, mental,
and spiritual power in usefulness to others.
—*Aristotle*

Happiness is like a kiss: To get any good out of it,
you must give it to somebody else.

There is one way of attaining happiness; it is by a sincere
and unrelaxing activity for the happiness of others.
—*Edward Bulwer-Lytton*

A general rule for happiness is: "Work a little harder;
work a little longer; work!"
—*Frederick H. Ecker*

If a man speaks or acts with pure thoughts,
happiness follows him like a shadow.
—*Buddha*

Happiness comes only when we push our brains and hearts to the farthest reaches of which we are capable.

—*Leo Rosten*

There is only one way to achieve happiness. And that is to have either a clear conscience, or none at all.

—*Ogden Nash*

Happiness is having a scratch for each itch.

—*Ogden Nash*

The foolish man seeks happiness in the distance; the wise man grows it under his feet.

—*James Oppenheim*

Happiness or misery is in the mind. It is the mind that lives.

—*James Cobett*

To be of use in the world is the only way to be happy.

—*Hans Anderson*

Synthetic happiness is the most expensive.

—*Arnold H. Glasgow*

Real happiness is cheap enough, yet how dearly we pay for its counterfeit.

—*Hosea Ballou*

It is not how much we have, but how much we enjoy,
that makes happiness.
—*Charles Spurgeon*

The happiest people are those who are too
busy to notice whether they are or not.
—*William Feather*

An act of goodness is of itself an act of happiness.
No reward coming after the event can compare
with the sweet reward that went with it.
—*Maurice Maeterlinck*

Extremely happy and extremely unhappy
men are prone to grow hardhearted.
—*Montesquieu*

The grand essentials of happiness are: something to do,
something to love, and something to hope for
—*Chalmers*

A man who is contented with what he ***has*** done, will
never be famous for what he ***will*** do.
—*Fred Estabrook*

The time to be happy is now.

I do not understand what the man who
is happy wants, in order to be happier
—*Cicero*

You cannot prevent the birds of sorrow from flying over your head, but you can prevent them from building nests in your hair.
—*Chinese Proverb*

Like swimming, writing, or playing golf, happiness can be learned.
—*Dr. Boris Sokoloff*

We take greater pains to persuade others that we are happy, than in eneavoring to be so ourselves.
—*Oliver Goldsmith*

Happy is the man who early learns the wide chasm that lies between his wishes and his powers.
—*Goethe*

Happiness comes not so much by occasional good fortune, but by little advantages that occur every day.
—*B. Franklin*

Man is the artificer of his own happiness.
—*David Henry Thoreau*

—*Also see Pleasure & Contentment*

HATE

I shall allow no man to belittle my
soul by making me hate him.
—*Booker T. Washington*

Hatred is a coward's revenge for being intimidated.
—*George Bernard Shaw*

Hatred stirs up strife, but love conquers all sins.
—*Proverbs* 10:12

Hating people is like burning down
your own house to get rid of a rat.
—*Harry Emerson Fosdick*

A chip on the shoulder usually
indicates there is wood higher up.

Whatever you love, you are its master;
but whatever you hate, you are its slave.
—D. D. *Runes*

Take care that no one hates you justly.
—*Syrus*

Hate no one; hate their vices, not themselves.
—*John G. Brainard*

Hate the evil, and love the good.
—*Amos 5:15a*

Calvary's cross reveals both God's love for man,
and man's hatred of God. How ironic !

—*Also see Anger & Contempt*

HEALTH

A man too busy to take care of his health is like a
mechanic too busy to take care of his tools.
—*Spanish Proverb*

He who has health has hope,
and he who has hope has everything.
—*Proverb*

If you have no time for your health today,
you may have no health for your time tomorrow.

Health and cheerfulness mutually beget each other.
—*Joseph Addison*

Health lies in labor, and there is no
royal road to it but through toil.
—*Wendell Phillips*

Health is so necessary to all the duties as well
as pleasures of life, that the crime of
squandering it is equal to the folly.
—*Samuel Johnson*

Good humor is the health of the soul,
sadness is its poison.
—*Stanislau*

The only way for a rich man to be healthy is by
exercise and abstinence—to live as if he were poor.
—*Sir William Temple*

—*Also see* Hope & Cheerfulness

HELP

A good place to find a helping hand
is at the end of your arm.
—H.F. *Banks*

The more help a man has in his garden,
the less it belongs to him.
—*William* H. *Davis*

Down in their hearts, wise men know that
the only way to help yourself is to help others.
—*Elbert Hubbard*

If you can't help someone any other way,
you can always pray for him.

Even if it's a little thing, do something for those who have need of a man's help—something for which you get no pay but the priviledge of doing it. For remember, you don't live in a world all your own.
—*Albert Schweitzer*

The highest service we can perform for others
is to help them help themselves.
—*Horace Mann*

No one is so rich that he does not need
another's help; no one so poor as not to be
useful in some way to his fellow man.
—*Pope Leo* XIII

He who sees a need and waits to be asked for
help is as unkind as if he had refused it.
—*Dante*

No man who is not willing to help himself has
any right to apply to his friends, or to God.
—*Demosthenes*

The only real help is self-help.
—*Pestalozzi*

You cannot help men permanently by doing for them
what they could and should do for themselves.
—*Abraham Lincoln*

The vocation of every man &
woman is to help other people.
—*Tolstoi*

—*Also see Generosity*

HISTORY

To be ignorant of the past is to remain a child.
—*Cicero*

Learning history is easy; learning its lessons
seems almost impossibly difficult.
—*Nicholas Bentley*

All ages of ***belief*** have been great;
all of ***un***belief have been mean.
—*Ralph Waldo Emerson*

In the history of mankind, fanatacism
has caused more harm than vice.
—*Louis Kronenberger*

The history of man is inseparable
from the history of religion.
—U.S. *Supreme Court*, 1962

Human history is the sad result of
everyone looking out for himself.
—Julio Cortazar

History is a better guide than good intentions.
—Jeane Kirkpatrick

Those who cannot remember the
past are condemned to repeat it.
—George Santayana

—Also see Learning

HONESTY

Honor and honesty are derived
from the same Latin word !!

Honesty is the first chapter in the book of Wisdom.

Following the path of least resistance is
what makes both rivers and men crooked.

Prefer loss before unjust gain; for that brings
grief but once; this forever.
—Chilo

Dishonesty is a forsaking of permanent
for temporary advantages.
—*Christian Bovee*

If honesty did not exist, we ought to
invent it as the best means of getting rich
—*Mirabeau*

All men's misfortunes proceed from their aversion
to being alone; hence gambling, extravagance,
wine, women, dissipation, ignorance, slander, envy,
and forgetfulness of what we owe to God.
—*Jean de la Bruyere*

Let him that stole steal no more; but rather let him
labor, working with his hands the thing which is good,
that he may have to give to him that needeth.
—*Ephesians* 4:28

The unrighteous shall not inherit the kingdom of
God. Be not deceived: neither fornicators, nor
idolators, nor adulterers, nor effeminate, nor
abusers of themselves with men, nor thieves, nor
the coveteous, nor drunkards, nor revilers, nor
extortioners, shall inherit the kingdom of God.
—I *Corinthians* 6:9

—*Also see* Integrity, Lies, & Truth

HONOR

No person was ever honored for what he received—
only for what he gave.
—*Calvin Coolidge*

Be honorable yourself, if you wish to
associate with honorable people.
—*Welsh Proverb*

Our own heart, and not other men's opinion,
forms our true honor.
—*Samuel Taylor Coleridge*

If I lose mine honor, I lose myself.
—*Shakespeare*

Honor the Lord with thy substance,
and with the first fruits of thine increase.
—*Proverbs* 3:9

Poverty and shame will come to him who disdains
correction, but he who regards reproof will be honored.
—*Proverbs* 13:18

The shortest and surest way to live with honor, is to be in reality what we would appear to be; all human virtues increase and strengthen themselves by the practice and experience of them.

—*Socrates*

—*Also see Respect*

HOPE

A misty morning doesn't signify a cloudy day.

Optimism is the faith that leads to achievement. Nothing can be done without hope.

There is always hope in a man who actually and earnestly works. In idleness alone is there perpetual despair.

—*Thomas Carlyle*

The dearest hope of the parent for his child is that he become all that he is capable of being. This should be the goal of school and college and exactly what city, state, and nation should strive for.

—*Morris Meister*

No one is hopeless who knows the God of hope.

—*Also see God*

HUMILITY

A humble man is like a good tree: the more fruit it bears, the more the branches bend down.

Sense shines with a double luster when it is set in humility. An able and yet humble man is a jewel worth a kingdom.
—*William Penn*

Whoever humbles himself like this child, is the greatest in the kingdom of heaven.
—*Matthew* 18:4 (NIV)

Humility leads to strength and not to weakness. It is the highest form of self-respect to admit mistakes and to make amends for them.
—*John J. McCloy*

Nothing is so humiliating than to see someone else succeed in efforts where we have tried but failed.
—*Flaubert*

Humility is to make a right estimate of one's self.
—*Charles Spurgeon*

Humility and the fear of the Lord
bring wealth and honor and life.
—*Proverbs* 22:4 (NIV)

—*Also see Confidence*

IDEAS

Daring ideas are like chessmen moved forward;
they may be beaten, but they may start a winning game.
—*Goethe*

A cold in the head causes less suffering than an idea.
—*Jules Renard*

Every time a man puts a new idea across,
he faces a dozen men who thought of it before he did—
but they only ***thought*** of it.
—*Oren Arnold*

Many ideas grow better when transplanted into another
mind than in the one where they sprang up.
—*Oliver Wendell Holmes*

An idea isn't responsible for the
people who believe in it.
—*Dan Marquis*

We often refuse to accept an idea merely
because the tone of voice in which it has
been expressed is unsympathetic to us.
—*Nietzche*

Everybody calls "clear" those ideas which have the
same degree of confusion as his own.
—*Marcel Proust*

If you really care about ideas, you will gather them
from every source and test them in every way.

—*Also see Minds & Thought*

IDLENESS

Idleness and pride tax with a heavier
hand than kings and parliaments.
—*Benjamin Franklin*

Too many folks fashion their life like
French bread—one long loaf.

Do not allow idleness to deceive you; for while you give him today, he steals tomorrow from you.
—*Alfred Crowquill*

In idleness there is perpetual despair.
—*Thomas Carlyle*

If you are idle, you are on the way to ruin, and there are few stopping places upon it. It is a precipice rather than a road.
—*Henry Ward Beecher*

Idleness is only the refuge of weak minds, and the holiday of fools.
—*Lord Chesterfield*

Leisure permits one to choose his own work. It does ***not*** infer the priviledge of idleness.
—*John Lubbock*

Slothfulness casteth into a deep sleep; and an idle soul shall suffer hunger.
—*Proverbs* 19:15

Shun idleness; it is rust that attaches itself to the most brilliant metals
—*Voltaire*

—*Also see Leisure & Laziness*

IGNORANCE

The more we study, the more we discover our ignorance.

Behind every argument is someone's ignorance.
—*Louis D. Brandeis*

Nothing is worse than watching ignorance in action.
—*Goethe*

Ignorance is voluntary misfortune.
—*Nicholas Lang*

He that is not aware of his ignorance
will only be misled by his knowledge.
—*Richard Whatley*

He fancies himself enlightened, because he sees the deficiencies of others; he is ignorant, because he has never reflected on his own.
—*Edward Bulwer-Lytton*

Whenever you argue with another wiser than yourself so others may admire your wisdom, they will discover your ignorance.
—*Saadi*

Ignorance, when voluntary, is criminal, and a man may be properly charged with that evil which he neglected, or refused to learn to prevent.
—*Samuel Johnson*

Everybody is ignorant, only on different subjects.
—*Will Rogers*

—*Also see Learning & Knowledge*

INDUSTRY

There is no substitute for work.
—*Henry Ford*

Life gives nothing to man without labor.
—*Horace*

When work is hardest, is the very hour when you need to work hardest.
—F.D.*VanAmburgh*

If hard work is not genius, it is the best possible substitute for it.
—*James A. Garfield*

Work is often the father of pleasure.
—*Voltaire*

The man who watches the clock, usually remains a hand.

Too many people quit looking for work,
when they get a job.

Without labor, nothing prospers.
—*Sophocles*

When you play, play hard; when you work,
don't play at all.
—*Theodore Roosevelt*

Labor disgraces no man; unfortunately,
you occasionally find men disgrace labor.
—*Ulysses S. Grant*

The average person puts only 25% of his energy and ability into his work. The world takes off its hat to those who put in more than 50% of their capacity, and stands on its head for those who devote 100%.
—*Andrew Carnegie*

The returns from hard work are like the
income from a safe investment—
the return may be modest but it is sure.
—*William Feather*

Labor is the great producer of wealth;
it moves all other causes.
—*Daniel Webster*

Honest industry always travels the same road
with enjoyment and duty, and progress is
altogether impossible without it.
—*Samuel Smiles*

Work is love made visible.
—*Kahlil Gibran*

If we would have anything of benefit,
we must earn it, and earning it becomes
shrewd, inventive, active, and enterprising.
—*Henry Ward Beecher*

I pity the creature who doesn't work, at whichever end of
the social scale he may regard himself as being.
—*Theodore Roosevelt*

The man who does his work, any work, conscientiously,
must always be in one sense a great man.
—*Dinah Mulock*

He who never does more than he is paid to do,
will never be paid for more than he does.

There are many ways of being frivolous, but only one way of being intellectually great; that is honest labor.

—*Sydney Smith*

The person who studiously avoids work usually works far harder than the man who pleasantly confronts it and does it. Men who cannot work hard are not happy men.

—*L. Ron Hubbard*

Industry is fortune's right hand, and frugality her left.

—*John Ray*

Genius may conceive,
but patient labor must consummate.

—*Harace Mann*

The fruit derived from labor is the
sweetest of all pleasures.

—*Marquis de Vanvenargues*

He who labors diligently never need despair;
for all things are accomplished by diligence and labor.

—*Menander*

Nothing is so difficult but it may be won by labor.

—*Terence*

Next to faith in God is faith in labor.

—*Christian Bovee*

Industry can do anything which genius can do,
and very many things which it cannot.
—*Henry Ward Beecher*

If you want knowledge, you must toil for it; if good, you must toil for it; and if pleasure, you must toil for it. Toil is the law. Pleasure comes through toil, and not by self-indulgence and indolence. When one gets to love his work, his life is a happy one.
—*John Ruskin*

Few of us get anything without working for it.
—*William Feather*

The bee, from her industry in the summer,
eats honey all winter long.

If any would not work, neither should he eat.
—II *Thessalonians* 3:10

Concentration is my motto—first honesty,
then industry, then concentration.
—*Andrew Carnegie*

It is not enough to be industrious; so are the ants.
What are you industrious *about*?
—*Thoreau*

The three great essentials to achieve
anything worthwhile are: first, hard work;
second, stick-to-itiveness; and third, common sense.
—*Thomas A Edison*

With industry, nothing is impossible.
—*Latin Proverb*

Anything of real benefit must be earned. Relatively few
people get anything without working for it.

Every man shall receive his own reward
according to his own labor.
—I *Corinthians* 3:8*b*

To live well is to work well,
to show a good activity.
—*Thomas Aquinas*

Do not muzzle the ox that treads out the corn;
the laborer is worthy of his reward.
—I *Timothy* 5:18

—*Also see* Economy & Wealth

INGENUITY

For every problem the Lord has made, He has also made a solution. If we can't find the solution, then let's honestly admit that we are fools. Why blame it on the Lord and say He created something "impossible".

—*Thomas A. Edison*

Genius is the power to labor better and more availably.

—*Ralph Waldo Emerson*

Genius is 2% inspiration and 98% perspiration.

—*Thomas A. Edison*

The highest genius is willingness and ability to do hard work. Any other conception of genius makes it a doubtful, if not a dangerous possession.

—*Rober A.MacArthur*

—*Also see Talent*

INTEGRITY

Law and justice are inseparable from moral integrity.

Integrity begins with a person being
willing to be honest with himself.
—*Cort* R. *Flint*

The just man walketh in his integrity;
his children are blessed after him.
—*Proverbs* 20:7

One thing you can give, but still keep, is your word.

He who values God's word will keep his own word.
—*Our Daily Bread*

A little integrity is better than any career.

Nothing baffles those who are full of tricks
and duplicity, more than straightforward
and simple integrity in another.
—*Colton*

Integrity without knowledge is weak and useless, and
knowledge without integrity is dangerous and dreadful.
—*Samuel Johnson*

Let integrity and uprightness preserve me.
—*Psalm* 25:21*a*

—*Also see Character, Honesty, Truth, & Virtue*

JUDGEMENT

In case of dissention, never dare to
judge till you've heard the other side.
—*Euripedes*

One cool judgement is worth a thousand hasty
councils. The thing to do is to supply light, not heat.
—*Woodrow Wilson*

We judge ourselves by what we feel ***capable*** of doing,
while others judge us by what we have ***already done***.
—*Henry Wadsworth Longfellow*

It was the vigorous pronouncements Jesus made
on controversial matters that sent Him to the
cross. Had he confined Himself to Mickey Mouse
morals, He would never have been heard of.
—*Dr. E. T. Dahlberg*

We judge ourselves by our ***motives***,
and others by their ***actions***.
—*Dwight Morrow*

A man with a surplus can control circumstances,
but a man without a surplus is controlled by them,
and often has no opportunity to exercise judgement.
—*Harvey Firestone*

He that judges without informing
himself to the utmost that he is capable,
cannot acquit himself of judging amiss.
—*John Locke*

We ought not to judge men's merits by their
qualifications, but by the use they make of them.
—*Charron*

Judgement is the treasure of a wise man. He that
has more knowledge than judgement is made for
another man's use more than his own.
—*William Penn*

Why do you judge or look down on your brother?;
for we all shall stand before the judgement seat of God.
—*Romans* 14:10

—*Also see Discretion, Perspective, & Prejudice*

JUSTICE

I tremble for my country when I reflect that God is just !
—*Thomas Jefferson*

Justice is inseparable from moral integrity.

Justice is what many people cry for when
they really want revenge.

Justice is not created by laws,
but laws should reflect and uphold justice.

—*Also see Integrity*

KINDNESS

It takes only a moment to be kind,
but the result can last forever
—*Our Daily Bread*

One of the most difficult things to give away is
kindness—because usually it is returned.
—C. R. *Flint*

Wherever there's a human being,
there's an opportunity for a kindness.
—*Seneca*

Persistent kindness conquers the ill-disposed.
—*Cicero*

Being kind is more important than being right.

We've not yet begun to use kind words as
abundantly as they should to be used.
—*Blaise Pascal*

The best portion of a good man's life is his little,
nameless, unremembered acts of kindness and love.
—*William Wordsworth*

Kindness is like snow—
It will make beautiful anything it covers.

If we expect a return for a favor,
it is not a gift, but a trade.

Truth generally is kindness, but where the two diverge
and collide, kindness should override truth.
—*Samuel Butler*

The greatest pleasure I know is to do a good action by
stealth and to have it discovered by accident.
—*Charles Lamb*.

The joy of a man is his kindness.
—*Proverbs* 19:22

The only real way to help yourself is to help others.

Let him who bestows the benefit conceal it;
let him who receives it, reveal it.
—*Seneca*

—*Also see Love & Generosity*

KNOWLEDGE

To be conscious that you are ignorant
is a great step to knowledge.
—*Benjamin Disraeli*

Far more crucial than what we know
or don't know, is what we don't ***want*** to know.
—*Eric Hoffer*

It is better to ask some of the questions
than to know all the answers.
—*James Thurber*

The man who thinks he knows everything about a subject renounces all
hope of learning anything more about it.
—*William J. Stevens*

The fear of the Lord is the beginning of knowledge.
—*Proverbs 1:7a*

Every branch of knowledge which a good man
possesses, he may apply to some good purpose.
—*Claudius Buchanan*

The only persons who achieve much are those
who want knowledge so badly that they seek it
while the conditions are still unfavorable.
Favorable conditions never come.
—*C.S.Lewis*

Carelessness does more harm than want of knowledge.
—*Benjamin Franklin*

Knowledge of a few things is better
than guesswork at many.

No man is entirely unmoved by being
asked for information upon his particular subject.
—*Lord Dunsany*

Knowledge is a treasure but practice is the key to it.
—*Thomas Fuller*

Study without reflection is a waste of time;
and reflection without study is dangerous.
—*Confucius*

Fullness of knowledge always necessarily means some understanding of the depths of our ignorance, and that is always conducive to both humility and reverence.
—*Robert A. Millikan*

If a little knowledge is dangerous, where is the man who has so much as to be out of danger?
—*Thomas Huxley*

Knowledge without common sense is very unwise. If we do not understand what we learn, then our knowledge has absolutely no power.
—*J. Edgar Hoover*

Knowledge, once gained, casts a faint light beyond its own immediate boundaries. There is no discovery so limited as not to illuminate something beyond itself.
—*John Tyndall*

Knowledge is the only instrument of production that is not subject to diminishing returns.
—*J.M. Clark*

People don't care how much you know, until they know how much you care.

Knowledge without wisdom is folly.
—*Baltasar Gracian*

A good listener is not only popular everywhere,
but after a while he knows something.
—*Wilson Mizner*

As a general rule, the most successful man in life
is the man who has the best information.
—*Disraeli*

The end of all knowledge should be in virtuous action.
—*Phillip Sydney*

—*Also see Learning, Teaching, & Wisdom*

LAZINESS

The greater part of human misery
is caused by indolence.
—*Georg Lichtenberg*

A lazy man is never lucky.
—*Persian Proverb*

By nature's laws, immutable and just,
enjoyment stops where indolence begins.
—*Robert Pollok*

Indolence is the dry rot of even a good mind and a good character; the practical uselessness of both. It is the waste of what might be a happy and useful life.
—*Tryon Edwards*

Go to ant thou sluggard; consider her ways and be wise.
—*Proverbs 6:6*

—*Also see Leisure & Idleness*

LEADERSHIP

He who follows the crowd is always behind.

Leaders are ordinary persons with extraordinary determination
—*Herbert Kaufman*

Leaders who serve, will serve as good leaders.

No one can control others, until he first learns to control himself.

There are two kinds of leaders: Those who are interested in the flocks, and those who are interested in the fleece.

If a ruler pays attention to lies,
all his servants become wicked.
—*Proverbs* 29:12

Leadership is the art of getting others to want to do
something you are convinced ***should*** be done.
—*Vance Packard*

The leader must know, must know that he knows,
and must be able to make it abundantly clear to
those about him that he knows.
—*Clarence* B. *Randall*

A strong leader knows that developing his
associates makes him even stronger.
—J.F.*Lincoln*

It usually takes a very big man to delegate
responsibilities, then let others handle them. He will
give a free hand, and then watch results. He does not
actively supervise people, but very closely supervises the
results. The man who is afraid to deputize will retard
growth—both his, and his organization's.
—B.C.*Forbes*

The man who commands efficiently,
must have obeyed others in the past.
—*Cicero*

He that would govern others, must first become the master of himself, richly imbued with the depth of understanding and height of knowledge.
—*Phillip Massinger*

The hand of the diligent will rule,
but the slothful will be put to forced labor.
—*Proverbs* 12:24

—*Also see* Authority, Dictators, Duty, Government, & Power

LEARNING

It is what you learn after you think
you know it all, that counts.
—*Harry* S. *Truman*

The man who is afraid of asking is ashamed of learning.
—*Danish Proverb*

Cursed be all learning that is
contrary to the cross of Christ.
—*Jonathon Dickinson*, 1st *President of* Princeton University.

The man who has ceased to grow
intellectually has begun to go down.
—*William Mathews*

None is less eager to learn than those
who know nothing.

We learn to do, neither by thinking nor by doing; we
learn to do by thinking about what we are doing.
—*George D. Stoddard*

Example is a lesson that all men can read.
—*Gilbert West*

Being ignorant is not so much a
shame as being unwilling to learn.
—*Benjamin Franklin*

Learning is an ornament in prosperity, a refuge
in adversity, and a provision in old age.
—*Aristotle*

Education begins to do its full work only when the
materials of learning, ably and imaginatively presented,
penetrate into the very marrow of the learner and set up
there a process of desiring that will not be stilled.
—*Nathan* M. *Pusey*

He that learns but makes no use of it, is a
beast of burden with a load of books. Does
the ass comprehend whether he carries on
his back a library or a bundle of faggots ?
—*Saadi*

He who refuses instruction despises his own soul;
but he who hears reproof gets understanding.
—*Proverbs* 15:32

Whoever loves instruction loves knowledge,
but he who hates reproof is stupid.
—*Proverbs* 12:1

The time for extracting a lesson from history
is ever at hand for those who are wise.
—*Demosthenes*

One pound of learning requires ten pounds
of common sense to apply it.
—*Persian Proverb*

He who adds not to his learning, diminishes it.
—*The Talmud*

I am always ready to learn,
although I do not always like being taught.
—*Winston Churchill*

—*Also see* Ignorance, Knowledge, Teaching, & Wisdom

LEISURE

The difference between existence and
life is the intelligent use of leisure.

Easy street is a blind alley.
—*Wilson Mizner*

Leisure permits one to choose his own work.
It does ***not*** infer the priviledge of idleness.
—*John Lubbock*

—*Also see Idleness & Laziness*

LIBERTY

Eternal vigilance is the price of liberty.
—*Thomas Jefferson*

Liberty may be endangered as much by the **abuse** of it,
as it is by the abuse of power.
—*James Madison*

God grants liberty **only** to those who love it,
and are always ready to guard and defend it.
—*Daniel Webster*

Freedom is obtained not by the **enjoyment** of what is desired, but by **controlling** desire itself.
—*Epictetus*

Men are qualified for civil liberty in exact proportion to their disposition to put moral chains upon their own appetites.
—*Edmund Burke*

No man is free who is not master of himself.
—*Epictetus*

The greatest freedom is freedom from sin.
—*Our Daily Bread*

Men fight for freedom,
but then enact laws to take it away.

The principles of the Bible are the groundwork of human freedom.
—*Horace Greeley*

Those who expect to reap the blessings of freedom must, like a man, undergo the fatigue of supporting it.
—*Thomas Paine*

Defending the freedom of others defines those who are truly free; failure to do so defines those who are ready to be enslaved.
—*Alan Patton*

Freedom is the right to one's dignity as a man.
—*Archibald MacLeish*

Give me liberty or give me death.
—*Patrick Henry*

All might be free if they valued
freedom and defended it as they ought.
—*Samuel Adams*

He that would make his own liberty secure,
must guard even his enemy from oppression.
—*Thomas Paine*

Take heed, that by any means this liberty of yours
becomes a stumbling block to them that are weak.
—I *Corinthians* 8:9

Freedom is a noble objective only for
responsible individuals.
—*Milton Friedman*

It behooves every man who values liberty of conscience
for himself, to resist invasions of it in the case of others.
—*Thomas Jefferson*

Liberty lies in people's hearts; when it dies there, no
constitution, law, or court can save it.
—*Learned Hand*

Where the spirit of the Lord is, there is liberty.
—II *Corinthians* 3:17*b* (*The obvious corallary is that where the spirit of the* Lord *is* ***absent***, *people can* **not** *be free*)

Only ***good*** people can be free;
when ***bad*** men want freedom, they really seek ***license.***
—*John* Milton

Those who give up liberty for security
deserve ***neither*** liberty nor security.
—*Benjamin Franklin*

Only a virtuous people are capable of freedom. As nations become more corrupt and
vicious, they have more need of masters.
—*Benjamin Franklin*

Freedom without responsibility, can lead only to
anarchy or tyranny. After all, if men don't restrain
themselves, then someone else will.

—*Also see* Conscience & Responsibility

LIES

Lying lips are an abomination to the Lord;
but they that deal truly are his delight.
—*Proverbs* 12:22

The cruelest lies are often told in silence.
—*Robert Louis Stevenson*

There is no such thing as a free lunch.
—*Milton Friedman*

May God deliver us from the lies of honest men.
—*Proverb, author unknown*

He that says he knows Christ but doesn't
keep his commandments is a liar.
—*I John 2:4a*

—*Also see* Honesty, Integrity & Truth

LIFE

Only a life lived for others is worthwhile.
—*Albert Einstein*

If a man hasn't discovered something
he will die for, he isn't fit to live.
—*Martin Luther King, Jr.*

Some get out of life exactly what they
put into it—nothing.
—*Arnold Glasgow*

Life is like a jewel—the number of facets
determine its sparkle.

Reverence for life requires that we sacrifice
a portion of our own lives for others.
—*Albert Schweitzer*

Small is the gate and narrow is the road
that leads to life, and only a few find it.
—*Matthew* 7:14

Wish not so much to live long, as to live well.
—*Benjamin Franklin*

Life doesn't consist of getting good cards,
but in playing a poor hand well.

Our business in life is not to get ahead of others
but to get ahead of ourselves—to break our own
records, to outstrip our yesterdays by our todays,
to do our work with more force than ever before.
—*Stewart B. Johnson*

Utmost decency in all our dealings is the greatest
need of the hour. Besides being the proper thing,
in the long run it pays handsome dividends.
—*Albert B. Lord*

Every time a man smiles, but even more so when he laughs, it adds something to this fragment of life.

—*Laurence Stern*

We are here for just a spell and then pass on.
So get a few laughs and do the best you can.

Live your life so that whenever you lose it you are ahead.

—*Will Rogers*

Those who are prepared to die, are prepared to live.

Don't let life discourage you; everyone who got where he is had to begin where he was.

—*Richard L. Evans*

Life without worthy ideals is wholly unsatisfying—sour.

—*B.C. Forbes*

Man cannot enjoy life by comparing it with that of his brother.

Although most Americans are gracious, warm, and generous, the upper income group seem sort of frosty—always looking over their shoulders to see who's watching, afraid they might not be in vogue.

—*Louis Harris*

Life is a pretty wonderful thing. You can't sit down and let it lap around you. You have to plunge into it; you have to dive through it!

The secret of life is not in what ***happens*** to you, but in what you ***do*** with what happens to you.
—*Norman Vincent Peale*

Wherever our life touches yours, you make us stronger or weaker. There is no escape. Man drags man down, or man lifts man up.
—*Booker* T. *Washington*

A man has made at least a start on discovering the meaning of human life when he plants shade trees under which he knows he will never sit.
—*Elton Trueblood*

He who asks of life nothing but the improvement of his own nature, and a continual moral progress toward inward content and religious submission, is less liable than anyone else to miss and waste life.
—*Frederic Amiel*

The best things in life are never rationed. Friendship, loyalty, love, do not require coupons.
—*George* T. *Hewitt*

Life's greatest achievement is the continual re-making of yourself so that at last you know how to live.
—*Winfred Rhodes*

To be spiritually-minded is life and peace.
—*Romans 8:6b*

Life is God's gift to us.
What we do with it, is our gift to God.

—*Also see Aim, Ambition, Failure, Luck, & Success*

LIGHT

There are two ways of spreading light; to be the candle, or the mirror that reflects it.
—*Edith Wharton*

I am the light of the world; he that followeth me shall not walk in darkness, but shall have the light of life.
—*John 8:12*

God is light, and in Him is no darkness at all.
—*I John 1:5b*

Light has come into the world, but men loved darkness instead of light because their deeds were evil. Everyone who does evil hates the light, and will not come into the light because his deeds will be exposed. But whoever lives by the truth comes to the light, so that it may be seen plainly that what he has done has been done through God.

—*John* 3:19-21

If we walk in the light, as He is in the light, we have fellowship with one another, and the blood of Jesus Christ, his Son, cleanses us from all sin.

—I *John* 1:7

Let your light so shine before men, that they may see your good works, and glorify your Father which is in heaven.

—*Matthew* 5:16

—*Also see* Belief & God

LOVE

Where there is room in the heart, there is always room in the house.

—*Thomas Moore*

Love and a cough cannot be hidden.
—*George Herbert*

Those who need love the most,
are those who least deserve it.

If you wish to be loved, be modest; if you wish to be admired, be proud; if you wish both, combine external modesty with internal pride.
—*Will Durant*

Love is patient, and kind. It does not envy or boast. It is not proud, rude, or self-seeking. It is not easily angered, and keeps no records of wrongs. It does not delight in evil, but rejoices with the truth. It always protects, trusts, hopes, and perseveres.
—*I Corinthians* 13: 4-7 (NIV, *paraphrased*)

The love of liberty is the love of others;
the love of power is the love of ourselves.
—*William Hazlitt*

We are all born for love; it is the principle
of existence and its only end.
—*Benjamin Disraeli*

Let us not love in word, neither in tongue;
but in deed and in truth.
—*I John* 3:18

There is no remedy for love but to love more.
—*David Henry Thoreau*

Where love rules, there is no will to power; and where power predominates, love is lacking. The one is the shadow of the other.
—*Carl Jung*

Love one another, as I have loved you.
—*John* 13:34

God is love.
—I *John* 4:8*b*

—*Also see Kindness & Generosity*

LOYALTY

Loyalty cannot be coerced or compelled, it has to be won.
—A. *Whitney Griswold*

There is no more important duty than loyalty to one's best convictions.
—*Edwin Chapin*

No man can serve two masters; for either he
will hate the one and love the other, or else
he will hold to the one and despise the other.
You cannot serve both God and riches.
—*Matthew* 6:24

If someone betrays you once, it is his fault;
if he betrays you twice, it is your fault.

—*Also see* Integrity

LUCK

Luck is the thing that happens when
preparation meets opportunity.

Shallow men believe in luck.
Strong men believe in cause and effect.
—*Emerson*

Hope nothing from luck, and the probability is that
you will be so prepared, forewarned, and forearmed,
that all shallow observers will call you lucky.
—*Edward Bulwer-Lytton*

Good luck is another name for tenacity of purpose.
—*Emerson*

I am luckiest with the potatoes that I hoe the most.

There may be luck in getting a good job,
but there's no luck in keeping it.
—*J.Ogden Armour*

The fortunate circumstances of our lives are generally
found, at last, to be of our own producing.
—*Oliver Goldsmith*

A lazy man is never lucky.
—*Persian Proverb*

Chance favors the prepared mind.
—*Louis Pasteur*

I believe in luck, because the harder
I work the more of it I have.
—*Stephen Leacock*

Luck comes once in a while,
trained efficiency comes all the time.

—*Also see Chance, Risk, & Safety*

MAN

Men are like trains. They operate
best when they are on the level.

We are all manufacturers—making good,
making trouble, or making excuses.
—*H.V. Adolt*

One cannot always be a hero,
but one can always be a man.
—*Goethe*

There is only a small difference between men;
but that small difference makes a big difference.
—*Arnold Glasgow*

Every individual has a place to fill in the
world, and is important in some respect,
whether he chooses to be or not.
—*Nathaniel Hawthorne*

For a man to achieve all that is demanded of him, he
must regard himself as greater than he is.
—*Goethe*

A superior man is the one who
is free from fear and anxieties.
—*Confucius*

A man has to live with himself, and he should see
to it that he always has good company.
—*Charles Evans Hughes*

No man can consistently wear one face to himself
and another to the multitude, without finally getting
bewildered as to which of those may be true.
—*Nathaniel Hawthorne*

Men are not against you; they are merely for themselves.
—*Gene Fowler*

No man ever did an injury to another, but at
the same time he did a greater injury to himself.
—*Henry Horne*

Men become bad and guilty because they speak and act
without foreseeing the results of their words and deeds.
—*Franz Kafka*

The doctrine of human equality reposes on this:
That there is no man really clever who has not
found that he is stupid. There is no big man who
has not felt small. Some men never feel small, but
those are the few men who really are.
—*Gilbert K. Chesterton.*

The man who can put himself in the place of other men, who can understand the workings of their minds, need never worry about what the future has in store for him.

—*Owen D. Young*

Better a man who knows his own stupidities, than the man who's too sure of everything.

—*Stephen Becker*

I love the man who can smile in trouble, that can gather strength from distress, and grow brave by reflection.

—*Thomas Paine*

If a man has good manners and is not afraid of other people, he will get by—even is he is stupid.

—*Sir David Eccles*

To become a thoroughly good man, is the best prescription for keeping a sound mind in a sound body.

—*Frances Bowen.*

—*Also see People*

MARRIAGE

Man's best possession is a sympathetic wife.

—*Euripedes*

Marriage is three parts love and
seven parts forgiveness of sins.
—*Langdon Mitchell*

To marry a woman for her beauty
is like buying a house for its paint.

Marriage is an adventure in cooperation. The
more we share, the richer we become; the
less we share, the poorer we will be.
—*Harold* B. *Walker*

When a man declares, "I am sure of my wife", it means
he is sure of his wife. But when a woman says, "I am sure
of my husband", it means that she is sure of herself.
—*Francis de* Croisset

Marriage should be honored by all,
and the marriage bed kept pure.
—*Hebrews* 13;*4a*

Marriage is the only accurate definition of "safe sex".

—*Also see* Children & Family

MATURITY

Growing old is mandatory; growing up is optional. **Do it**.

To grow up in life means learning to
live with impossible problems.
—*Blaine McLaughlin*

The mark of an immature man is that he wants to
die nobly for a cause, while the mark of a mature
man is that he wants to live humbly for one.
—*Wilhelm Steckel*

MEMORY

Bad memory is rooted in bad attention.

No man has a good enough memory
to make a successful liar.
—*Abraham Lincoln*

We have committed The Golden Rule to memory.
Let us now commit it to life.
—*Edward Markham*

A retentive memory may be a good thing , but the ability
to forget is the true token of greatness.
—*Elbert Hubbard*

—*Also see* Minds

MINDS

Small minds dwell on ***things***. Average minds dwell on
people, things, and events. But great minds dwell on
ideas—and how those ideas can impact people,
things, and events for the better.

Some minds are like concrete—
thoroughly mixed and permanetly set.

The Bible was written for men with a
head on their shoulders.
—*Martin Luther*

A person's mental capacity is better determined
by his questions, than by his answers.

A weak mind is like a microscope, which magnifies
trifling things but cannot receive great ones.
—*Lord Chesterfield*

The mind is like a trunk. If well packed, it holds almost everything; if ill-packed, it holds almost nothing.
—*Agustus T. Hare*

Minds are like parachutes.
They only function when they are open.
—*Thomas Dewar*

Never be so open-minded that
you let all of your brains fall out.

Only dead men never change their minds.

Every human mind is a great slumbering
power, until awakened by a keen desire
and by definite resolution to do.
—*Edgar F. Roberts*

Unless a capacity for thinking be accompanied by a capacity for action, a superior mind exists in torture.
—*Benedetto Croce*

Narrow minds think nothing right
that is above their own capacity.
—*La Rouchefoucauld*

Happiness or misery is in the mind.
It is the mind that lives.
—*Willaim Cobbett*

A mind in motion is like a rolling snowball.
—*Edward* O'*Blenis*

Everyone should keep a mental wastebasket, and the older we grow the more things we should consign to it.
—*Samuel* Butler

The mind of a bigot is like the pupil of the eye; the more light you pass upon it, the more it will contract.
—*Oliver* Wendell Holmes

A wide mouth often results from a narrow mind.

Your brain is the nearest gold mine. Keep digging!
—F.E.*Churchill*

The greater intellect one has, the more originality one finds in men. Ordinary persons find no difference between men.
—*Blaise Pascal*

Be not conformed to this world, but be transformed by the renewing of your mind, that ye may prove that which is good, acceptable, and perfect will of God.
—*Romans* 12:2

The mind is the great lever of all things.
—*Daniel Webster*

—*Also see* Ideas, Memory, & Thought

MISTAKES

Mistakes comprise the discipline
through which we advance.
—*William Ellery Channing*

An error becomes a ***mistake***,
only when you refuse to correct it.

A man who commits a mistake but doesn't correct it,
is making another mistake.
—*Confucius*

Never be ashamed to say you've been wrong, because it
only reveals that you are wiser today than yesterday.
—*Alexander Pope*

There is no greater mistake than the hasty
conclusion that opinions are worthless
because they are badly argued.
—*Thomas Huxley*

Half our mistakes in life arise from feeling where we
ought to think, and thinking where we ought to feel.
—*John Churton Collins*

It is more important to know where you
are going than to get there quickly. Do
not mistake activity for achievement.
—*Mabel Newcomber*

Learn from the mistakes of others. You can't live long
enough to make them all yourself.To get maximum
attention, it's hard to beat a big mistake.

—*Also see Failure*

MONEY

Money is a good servant, but a bad master.

He who can afford to gamble, doesn't need money;
he who needs money, can't afford to gamble.

No man's credit is as good as his money.
—*Edgar W. Howe*

The use of money is all there is in having it.
—*Benjamin Franklin*

Whenever money is the principle object of life with
either man or nation, it is both ill- gotten and ill-spent;
and it does harm both in the getting and the spending.
—*John Ruskin*

Money is of a prolific generating nature. Money can beget money, and its offspring can beget more.
—*Benjamin Franklin*

Money and time are the heaviest burdens of life, and the unhappiest of all mortals are those who have more of either than they know how to use.
—*Samuel Johnson*

The darkest hour in the history of any young man is when he sits down to study how to get money without honestly earning it.
—*Horace Greeley*

Two things are as big as the man who possesses them—neither bigger nor smaller. One is a minute; the other is a dollar.
—*Channing Pollock*

I suppose there is not a man in the world who, when he becomes a knave for the sake of a thousand dollars, would not rather have remained honest for half that much.
—*G.C. Lichtenberg*

They who are of the opinion that money will do everything, may very well be suspected of doing anything for money.
—*George Savile*

The art of living easily as to money, is to pitch your scale of living one degree below your means.

—Henry Taylor

To lose money ill is often a crime; but to get it ill is a worse one, and to spend it ill, is worst of all.

—Ruskin

Only one man in a thousand understands the currency question, and we meet him every day.

—Kin Hubbard

No money can buy the needs of the soul.

The ***love*** of money is the root of all evil.

—I Timothy 6:10a

—Also see Wealth

MOTHERS

A mother, who is really a mother, is never free.

—Honore de Balzac

By and large, mothers and housewives are the
only workers who don't have regular time off.
They are the vacationless class.
—*Anne Morrow Lindberg*

God could not be everywhere, so He created mothers.
—*Jewish Proverb*

—*Also see Children & Family*

MOTIVES

He who is sure of his motives
can advance or retreat with confidence.
—*Goethe*

He that diligently seeketh good, procureth favor;
but he that seeketh mischief, it shall come unto him.
—*Proverbs* 11:27

Few things are impossible to diligence & skill
—*Samuel Johnson*

The road to hell is paved with good intentions.
—*English Proverb*

—*Also see Aim & Purpose*

OPINIONS

One man likes to say what he knows,
another what he thinks.
—*Joseph Joubert*

The man who questions opinions is wise;
the man who quarrels with facts is a fool.
—*Frank A. Garbutt*

The world is divided into people
who think they are right.

New opinions are always suspected, and
usually opposed, without any other reason
but because they are not already common.
—*John Locke*

Our opinions become fixed at the point
where we stop thinking.
—*Joseph Ernest Renan*

Obstinacy and vehemence in opinion
are the surest proofs of stupidity.
—*Bernard Barton*

Inconsistencies of opinion, arising from
changes of circumstances, are often justifiable.
—*Daniel Webster*

There is nothing on which men are commonly more intent than on making a way for their opinions.
—*Michel de Montaigne*

We are like sheep; we wait to see how the drove is going, then go with the drove. We have two opinions; one private, which we are afraid to express; and another one—the one we use—which we force ourselves to wear to please Mrs. Grundy, until habit makes us comfortable in it, and the custom of defending it makes us love it, adore it, and forget how pitifully we came by it. Look at it in Politics.
—*Mark Twain*

There is no greater mistake than the hasty conclusion that opinions are worthless because they are badly argued.
—*Thomas Huxley*

A true gentleman doesn't make an issue out of every difference of opinion.
—*Arnold H. Glasgow*

—*Also see Ideas & Thought*

OPPORTUNITY

I will study and prepare myself,
and then someday my chance will come.
—*Abraham Lincoln*

A wise man will ***make*** more opportunities than he ***finds***.
—*Francis Bacon*

Never mind your limitations; grasp your possibilities.

No great man ever complains about want of opportunity.
—*Ralph Waldo Emerson*

The opportunity God sends seldom
wakes up the one who is sleeping.
—*Senegalese Proverb*

Your ship won't come in unless you row out to meet it.

You'll never have a second chance
to make a good first impression.

He who waits for something to turn up,
should start with his shirtsleeves.

Opportunity often comes disguised as hard work.

Strange as it may seem, a man does not cut much ice unless he makes hay while the sun shines.

To each is given a bag of tools, a shapeless mass, and a book of rules. And each must make, ere life is flown, a stumbling block, or a stepping stone.
—R.L. *Sharp*

Next to knowing when to seize an opportunity, the most important thing is to know when to forego an advantage.
—*Benjamin Disraeli*

There is no security on this earth; there is only opportunity.
—*Dougas MacArthur*

A man in earnest finds means, or, if he cannot find, creates them.
—*William Ellery Channing*

Opportunities should never be lost, because they can hardly be regained.
—*William Penn*

Human felicity is produced not so much by great pieces of good fortune that seldom happen, as by little advantages that occur every day.
—*Benjamin Franklin*

Most of us never recognize opportunity until it
goes to work in our competitor's business.
—*P.L.Andarr*

While we stop to think, we often miss our opportunity.
—*Publius Syrus*

Don't be so busy doing small things that you fail
to see the opportunity to do large ones.

Mastery provides a shortcut to opportunity.

Opportunity is simply another name for your mental
attitude. It's all in the way you feel about things.

One type of opportunity is as common today as ever,
and that's the opportunity to improve ourselves.
—*William Feather*

Opportunity rarely knocks until you are ready.
And few people have ever been really ready
without receiving opportunity's call.
—*Channing Pollock*

Things don't turn up in this world,
until somebody turns them up.
—*James A. Garfield*

Capacity never lacks opportunity. It cannot remain undiscovered because it is sought by too many anxious to use it.

—*Cochran*

The way to miss success is to miss the opportunity

—*Victor Chasles*

—*Also see Character, Integrity, & Virtue*

PATIENCE

Patience is a necessary ingredient of genius.

—*Benjamin Disraeli*

All things come to him who waits—if he labors while he waits, and knows what he is waiting for.

Patience is power; with time and patience, the mulberry leaf becomes silk.

—*Chinese Proverb*

The future belongs to him who knows how to wait.

—*Russian Proverb*

Patience is the ability to idle your engine, when you feel like stripping your gears.

The greatest and sublimest power is
often simple patience.
—Horace Bushnell

A handful of patience is worth more
than a bushel of brains.
—Dutch Proverb

No honors are too distant for the man who
prepares himself for them with patience.
—Jean de la Bruyere

Patience makes the final difference between
success and failure. All the greatest people have it
to an infinite degree, and the patient weak ones
always conquer the impatient strong.
—John Ruskin

The world belongs to the patient man.
—Italian Proverb.

He that has patience can have what he will.
—Benjamin Franklin

Have patience. All things are difficult
before they become easy.
—Saadi

There are many times and circumstances in life
when our strength is to sit still.
—*Tryon Edwards*

—*Also see Perseverance*

PEACE

Since the Armistice was signed on November 11, 1918
after World War I, the "war to end all wars", there have
been only a few minutes of peace each year.

You may either win your peace or buy it: You ***win*** it by
resisting evil, but you ***buy*** it by compromising with evil.
—*John Ruskin* (*And, if you buy it, what a dear price you must pay*)

When we can't find tranquility within ourselves, it is
useless to look for it elsewhere.
—*La Rouchefoucauld*

Nothing can bring you peace but yourself.
—*Emerson*

Thou wilt keep him in perfect peace, whose mind is
stayed on thee, because he trusteth in thee.
—*Isaiah 26:3*

And the peace of God, which passes all understanding, shall guard your hearts and thoughts through Jesus Christ.
—*Philippians* 4:7

Let the peace of Christ rule in your hearts.
—*Colossians* 3:15*a*

—*Also see Belief & God*

PEOPLE

Some people are like a blotter.
They soak it all up, but get it all backwards.

Cold, precise, perfect people, in order not to speak wrong, never speak at all, and in order to do no wrong, never do anything.
—*Henry Ward Beecher*

People never know each other until they have eaten a certain amount of salt together.
—*Aristotle*

The best schooling in the world is dealing with people.

Most people are good only so long as
they believe others to be so.
—*Friedrich Hebbel*

What is best for people is what they do for themselves.
—*Benjamin Franklin*

There are only two kinds of people who know what they are after: the Communist, and the convinced Christian. The rest of the world are amiable non-entities.
—*Dr. Geoffrey Fisher*

If the people around you are spiteful and callous and will not hear you, fall down before them and beg their foregiveness—for in truth you are to blame for their not wanting to hear you.
—*Feodore Dostoevski*

—*Also see* Man

PERSEVERANCE

The hen doesn't quit scratching
just because the worms are scarce.
—*J.P. Gerloffs*

We can do anything we want to
if we stick to it long enough.
—*Helen Keller*

Consider the postage stamp: It's usefulness consists of
its ability to stick to one thing until it gets there.
—*Josh Billings.*

A quitter never wins; and a winner never quits.

You'll never cross the ocean if you get
off the ship when it storms.
—*C. F. Kettering*

Genius, the power that dazzles mortal eyes,
is oft but perseverance in disguise.
—*William Willard Austin*

A little and a little, collected together, become a great
deal; the heap in the barn consists of single grains.
—*Saadi*

Big shots are only little shots that kept shooting.
—*Christopher Morley*

If some men don't get quick results, they lose interest.
Others plan ahead, move forward slowly, and stick
doggedly to the job regardless of delays and hard luck.
—*William Feather*

Don't let mistakes or wrong decisions discourage you. Just try faithfully to be right, and you will become more right each day.

—*Carlyle*

What we ever hope to do with ease, we must first learn to do with diligence.

—*Johnson*

Some men quit when they've almost reached the goal—while others obtain victory by exerting, at the last moment, more vigorous efforts than before.

—*Polybius*

There is only one proof of ability—results. Men with ability in action get results.

—*Harry F. Banks*

No bird soars too high if he soars with his own wings.

—*William Blake*

Every man who observes vigilantly, and resolves steadfastly, grows unconsciously into genius.

—*Edward Bulwer-Lytton*

The will to persevere is often the difference between failure and success.

—*David Sarnoff*

Diligence is the mother of good luck,
and God gives all things to industry.
—*Benjamin Franklin*

Perseverence and audacity generally win.
—*Dorothee Luzy*

Perseverance is the most overrated of traits, ***if*** it is unaccompanied by talent; beating your head against the wall is more likely to produce a concussion than a hole in the wall. A ***foolish*** consistency is the hobgoblin of little minds.
—*Emerson*

If your job is puny and your pay is low, and the glories you get are few, remember, my friend, that the sturdy oak was once a nut like you.

He conquers who endures.
—*Italian Proverb*

Life isn't easy for any of us, but so what? We must persevere, have confidence in ourselves, and believe we are gifted for something, and this thing, whatever the cost, must be attained.
—*Marie Curie*

I have not yet begun to fight.
—*John Paul Jones*

Tenacity is the only key that will
open the door of success
—*David Lloyd George*

God is with those who patiently persevere.
—*Arab Proverb*

—*Also see Accomplishment, Action, Ambition, & Patience*

PERSPECTIVE

The only difference between a rut
and a grave are in their dimensions.
—*Allen Glasgow*

The only difference between stumbling blocks
and stepping stones, is in how you use them.

An optimist laughs to forget;
a pessimist forgets to laugh.

An optimist sees opportunity in every calamity; a
pessimist sees calamity in every opportunity.

It isn't the size of the dog in the fight,
but the size of the fight in the dog, that counts.
—*Harry Howell*

We see things not as ***they*** are, but as ***we*** are.
—*H.M.Tomlinson*

What we see depends mainly on what we look for.
—*John Lubbock*

The man whose only tool is a hammer,
sees every problem as a nail.

He that plants thorns must never expect to gather roses.
—*Pilpay*

It makes all the difference whether you hear
an insect in the bedroom, or in the garden.
—*Robert Lynd*

It is hard for an empty sack to stand upright.
—*Benjamin Franklin*

That which is not good for the swarm,
is also not good for the bee.
—*Marcus Aurelius*

Bees that have honey in their mouths,
also have stings in their tails.

The slightest pain in your little finger causes
you more uneasiness and anxiety than the
destruction and death of millions of people.
—*Sven Hassel*

Nothing is so good as it seems beforehand.
—*George Eliot*

Only in quiet waters do things mirror themelves undistorted. Only in a quiet mind is an adequate perception of the world.
—*Hans Margolius*

We always think every other man's job is easier than our own. And the better he does it, the easier it looks.
—*Eden Phillpots*

Let everyone sweep in front of his own door, and the whole world will be clean.
—*Goethe*

Some people stop & buy an apple on the corner & walk away as if they had just solved the entire unemployment problem.

You can't appreciate home 'til you've left it, money 'til it's spent, your wife 'til she's joined a woman's club, nor Old Glory 'til you see it hanging on a broomstick on the shanty of a consul in a foreign town.
—O. *Henry*

—*Also see Choice, Discretion, & Judgement*

PHILOSOPHY

We must have respect for both our plumbers
and our philosophers, or neither our pipes or
our theories will hold water.
—*John W. Garner*

If a man makes himself a worm,
he must not complain when he is trodden on.
—*Kant*

The difference between existence and life,
is the intelligent use of leisure.
—*Rev. Herman S. Hughes*

Too many of us know the shortcuts,
and too few know or care where the path leads.
—*Charles H. Brower*

We see the causes we are hunting for,
and we are looking for what is already in our minds.
—B. S. *Keyes*

The forces of conformity are strong. Too many of us are still sitting it out instead of sweating it out. We haven't got the guts to stand up straight and dare to be square, because the opposite of square is round, and being round is much simpler. Responsibilities and problems roll off easily. We can just roll down the path, without any bumps, and stay in the middle—because thats where the most comfortable ruts are.

—*Charles H. Brower*

Search and see if there is not some place where you may invest your humanity.

—*Albert Schweitzer*

—*Also see Belief. Faith, Religion. & Salvation*

PLEASURE

Don't mistake pleasure for happiness. They are a different breed of dogs.

—*Josh Billings*

The greatest pleasure I have known is to do a good action by stealth, and to have it found out by accident.

—*Charles Lamb*

Indulge yourself in pleasures only insofar as they are necessary for the preservation of health.

—*Spinoza*

Don't bite at the bait of pleasure till
you know there is no hook beneath it.
—*Thomas Jefferson*

After pleasant scratching, comes unpleasant itching.
—*Danish Proverb*

The great pleasure in life is doing what
other people say you cannot do.
—*Walter Bagehot*

We enjoy thoroughly the pleasure that we give.
—*Alexander Dumas*

He that loveth pleasure shall be a poor man.
—*Proverbs 21:17a*

—*Also see Happiness & Contentment*

POPULARITY

Popularity is a crime when it is sought.
It is only a virtue when it is unsought.
—*Marquis of Halifax*

—*Also see Fame*

POVERTY

The most prevalent and most debilitating poverty, is poverty of thought. (And ***most*** of us spend ***far*** less time in ***true*** and ***meaningful*** thought than we should !!)

Being poor is a frame of mind.
Being broke is only temporary.
—*Mike Todd*

Poverty is half laziness.
—*Yugoslavian Proverb*

Give me neither poverty nor riches.
—*Proverbs* 30:8

—*Also see* Want

POWER

The attempt to combine power and wisdom has only rarely been successful, and then only for a short time.
—*Albert Einstein*

Power corrupts, and absolute power corrupts absolutely.
—*Lord Acton*

Power buries those who wield it.
—*The Talmud*

Responsibilities gravitate to the person who can shoulder them; power flows to the man who knows how.
—*Elbert Hubbard*

Most powerful is he who has himself in his own power.
—*Seneca*

The only power which can resist the power of fear, is love.
—*Alan Paton*

Power is not revealed by striking hard or often, but by striking true.
—*Honore de Balzac*

No power is strong enough to be lasting if it labors under the weight of fear.
—*Cicero*

Self-reverence, self-knowledge, and self-control lead to sovereign power.
—*Tennyson*

—*Also see Authority, Dictators, Government, Leadership, Strength*

PRAISE

Those who don't praise, will never be worthy of it.
—*T. Fuller*

A word of appreciation can often accomplish
what nothing else could accomplish.
—B.C. *Forbes*

Praise makes good men better and bad men worse.
—*Thomas Fuller*

The meanest, most contemptible kind of
praise is that which first speaks well of a man,
and then qualifies it with a "but."
—*Henry Ward Beecher*

—*Also see Flattery*

PRAYER

If you are too busy to pray, you are too busy.

Man is never higher than when
he is on his knees before God.

There is a big difference between
praying, and saying prayers.

If you want to pray better, you must pray more.
—*Mother Teresa*

Prayer doesn't change things; it changes ***people***—
who change ***things***.

Prayer does not change God,
but changes him who prays.
—*Soren Kierkegaard*

Those who pray only when in trouble,
at least know where to turn for help.

Our thanks should be as fervent for mercies received,
as our petitions for mercies sought.
—*Charles Simmons*

Pray to God, but keep rowing the boat.
—*Russian Proverb*

Do not pray for easy lives. Pray to be stronger
men. Do not pray for tasks equal to your
powers. Pray for powers equal to your tasks.
—*Phillips Brooks*

Let us pray to be so guided that we shall foster the brotherhood of man and thus contribute to creating the Kingdom of Heaven on earth for the enjoyment of the whole human race.

—B.C. *Forbes*

God, give us the grace to accept with serenity the things that cannot be changed, courage to change the things which should be changed, and the wisdom to distinguish the one from the other.

—*Reinhold Niebur*

Help me to live so that I can lie down at night with a clear conscience, and unhaunted by those to whom I may have brought pain. Help me to earn my meal ticket squarely and by doing unto others as I would have them do unto me. Deafen me to the tingle of tainted money. Blind me to the faults of others, and reveal to me my own. Guide me so that when I look at my wife, who is a blessing to me, I will have nothing to hide. Keep me young enought to laugh with little children, and to be considerate of old age. And comes the day of darkening shades, make the ceremony short and the epitaph simple: "Here lies a man".

—*Author Unknown*

Give us grace and strength to forbear and to persevere. Give us courage and gaiety and the quiet mind, spare us to our friends, and soften us to our enemies.
—*Robert Louis Stevenson*

—*Also see Belief & God*

PREJUDICE

Prejudice is the child of ignorance.
—*Hazlitt*

Prejudice is being down on something you are not up on.

Racial prejudice will cease only when we admit there is but ***one*** race—the ***human*** race.

—*Also see Perspective*

PRIDE

Pride is the stone over which many people stumble.

Egotism is the anesthetic that dulls the pain of stupidity.
—*Frank Leahy*

Pride, arrogance, the evil way,
and perverse speech do I hate.
—*Proverbs* 8:13*b*

Pride is the mask of someone's faults.
—*Hebrew Proverb*

Temper gets people into trouble,
but it is pride that keeps them there.

A proud man is seldom a grateful man,
for he never thinks he gets as much as he deserves.
—*Henry Ward Beecher*

Woe unto you when all men speak well of you.
—*Luke* 6:26*a*

The reward of a thing well done is to have done it.
—*Ralph Waldo Emerson*

Pride goeth before destruction,
and a haughty spirit before a fall.
—*Proverbs* 16:18

Pride that dines on vanity, also sups on contempt.
—Benjamin Franklin

A man's pride shall bring him low;
but honor shall uphold the humble in spirit.
—Proverbs 29:23

We can believe almost anything if it is
necessary to protect our pride.
—Dr. Douglas A. Thorn

When pride cometh, then cometh shame.
—Proverbs 11:2a

Pride is the spring of malice, the desire of revenge,
and of rash anger and contention.
—Robert Leighton

A vain man may become proud and imagine himself
pleasing to all when he is in reality a universal nuisance.
—Benedict Spinoza

The Lord will destroy the house of the proud.
—Proverbs 15:25a

—Also see Conceit, Selfishness, & Vanity

PRINCIPLE

It is easier to fight for one's principles
than it is to live up to them.
—*Adlai Stevenson*

Whoever shall introduce into public affairs the principles
of Christianity will change the face of the world.
—*Benjamin Franklin*

Also see Conviction

PROGRESS

There's a way to do it better—**FIND** it !!
—*Thomas A. Edison*

All progress has resulted from people
who took an unpopular position.
—*Adlai Stevenson*

Go as far as you can. When you get there,
you will see farther.

No man can wind up being superior
without beginning by being inferior.

Restlessness and discontent are the
first necessities of progress.
—*Thomas A. Edison*

Nothing in progress can rest on its original
plan. We might as well think of rocking a
grown man in the cradle of an infant.
—*Edmund Burke*

—*Also see Change*

PURPOSE

There is no road to success but through
a clear and strong purpose.
—*Theodore Munger*

Man cannot live without some great
purpose outside himself.
—*Austin Phillips*

Purpose is what gives life meaning.
—C.H. *Parkhurst*

Take time to think and to pinpoint
what's really important in your life.
—*Alexander Reid Martin.*

To be what we are, and to become what we are
capable of becoming, is the only end in life.
—*Robert Louis Stevenson*

Have a purpose in your life, and having it,
throw such strength of mind and muscle into
your work as God has given you.
—*Thomas Carlyle*

The secret of success is constancy of purpose
—*Disraeli*

Concentration is my motto—
first honesty, then industry, then concentration.
—*Andrew Carnegie*

What you make it to the interest of men, they will do.
—*Edmund Burke*

Practice yourself, for heaven's sake in little things;
and then proceed to greater.
—*Epictetus*

Nothing worthwhile ever happens quickly and easily.
You achieve only as you are determined to achieve,
and as you keep at it until you have achieved.
—*Robert H. Lauer*

Doing little things well is a step toward
doing big things better.
—*Harry F. Banks*

The world will always be governed by self-interest.
We should not try to stop this. We should try and
make the self-interest of cads a little more
coincident with that of decent people.
—*Samuel Butler*

Deliberate before you begin, then execute with vigor.
—*Sallust*

Providence has nothing good or high in store for one
who does not resolutely aim at something high or good.
A purpose is the eternal condition of success.
—*Theodore H. Munger*

—*Also see Aim & Motives*

REASON

If you will not hear reason,
she will surely rap your knuckles.
—*Benjamin Franklin*

Reason often makes mistakes,
but conscience never does.
—*Josh Billings*

He who establishes his argument by noise and command, shows that his reason is weak.
—*Michel de Montaigne*

He who will not reason is a bigot; he who cannot is a fool; and he who dares not is a slave.
—*William Drummond*

Emotion has taught mankind to reason.
—*Vanvenargues*

Habits work more constantly and with greater force than reason, which, when we have most need of it, is seldom fairly consulted, and more rarely obeyed.
—*John Locke*

He only employs his passion who can make no use of his reason.
—*Cicero*

I can stand brute force, but brute reason is quite unbearable. It is hitting below the intellect.
—*Oscar Wilde*

Common sense is the daughter of reason.
—H.W. *Shaw*

Never do the ***right*** thing for the ***wrong reason***,
and never do the ***wrong*** thing for the ***right reason***.

—*Also see Motives, Thought, & Wisdom*

RELIGION

Fervid atheism is usually a screen for repressed religion.
—*Wilhelm Stekel*

Religion is about man's search for God; Christianity is about God's search for man. ***What a difference*** **!!**

A life without religion is a life without principles, and a life without principles is like a ship without a rudder.
—*Mahatma Ghandi*

Science gives us knowledge, which is power; religion gives us wisdom, which is control.
—*Martin Luther King*

Science and religion are two sides of the same glass—through which we see darkly; then they finally focus together and reveal the truth.
—*Pearl Buck*

Men will wrangle for religion; write for it; fight for it;
die for it; anything but ***live*** for it.
—*Charles Caleb Colton*

It was a common saying among the Puritans
that brown bread and the Gospel are good fare.
—*Matthew Henry*

Business is religion, and religion is business. The
man who does not make a business of his religion
has a religious life of no force; and the man who
does not make a religion of his business has a
business life with no character.
—*Maltbie Babcock*

Give me a man who is capable of devotion to anything,
rather than a cold, calculating average of all the virtues.
—*Bret Harte*

The world is my country, all mankind are my brethren,
and to do good is my religion.
—*Thomas Paine*

Work for the Lord. The pay is small,
but the retirement benefits are out of this world.

—*Also see Belief, Faith, Philosophy, & Salvation*

REPUTATION

When men speak ill of you,
so live that nobody will believe them.
—Plato

Character lives in a man; reputation lives outside of him.
—J.G. Holland

A man is valued by what others say of him.

Associate yourself with men of good quality if you
esteem your own reputation;
for 'tis better to be alone than in bad company.
—George Washington

When your work speaks for itself, don't interrupt.
—Henry J. Kaiser

The way to gain a good reputation is to
endeavor to be what you desire to appear.
—Socrates

The only way to make ourselves admired
is to be what we expect to be thought.
—Socrates

—Also see Character

RESPECT

You will never learn to respect your fellow man
until you first learn to respect yourself.

The more things a man is ashamed of,
the more respectable he is.
—G.B.*Shaw*

Without self-respect there can be no genuine
success. Success won at the cost of self- respect is
not success—for what shall it profit a man if he
gain the whole world and lose his self-respect?
—B.C.*Forbes*

Though the Lord be high, he hath respect for the lowly;
but the proud he knoweth afar off.
—*Psalm* 138:6

—*Also see* Courtesy, Honor, & Fame

RESPONSIBILITY

Don't get up from the feast of life
without paying for your share of it.
—W.R. *Inge*

Ability involves responsibility.
—*Alexander MacLaren*

In your area of responsibility, if you do not control events, you are at the mercy of events.
—*Harland Svare*

My only fear is that I shall not know all my duty, or shall fail to do it.
—*Mary Lyon*

It's easy to dodge responsibility, but you can't dodge the consequences of dodging it.
—*Sir Josiah Stamp*

Responsibility walks hand in hand with capacity and power.
—*J.G. Holland*

Every one of us shall give account of himself to God.
—*Romans* 14:12

Service is the rent that we pay for our room on earth.
—*Lord Halifax*

Practice yourself, for heaven's sake in little things; and then proceed to greater.
—*Epictetus*

—*Also see* Duty, & Leadership

RIGHTEOUSNESS

I am inferior to any man whose rights
I trample under foot.
—*Horace Greeley*

In the house of the righteous is much treasure;
but in the revenues of the wicked is trouble.
—*Proverbs* 15:6

Righteous people consider themselves sinners,
and sinners consider themselves righteous.
—*Pascal*

Treasures of wickedness profit from nothing;
but righteousness delivers from death.
—*Proverbs* 10:2

He that walks uprightly walks surely;
but he that perverts his ways shall be known.
—*Proverbs* 10:9

Righteousness exalts a nation;
sin is a reproach to any people.
—*Proverbs* 14:34

Whoever walks uprightly shall be saved;
but he that is perverse in his ways shall fall at once.
—*Proverbs* 28:18

Seek ye first the kingdom of God, and his righteousness,
and all these things shall be added unto you.
—*Matthew* 6:33

And if the righteous scarcely be saved, where
shall the ungodly and the sinner appear ?
—I *Peter* 4:18

He that keeps Christ's commandments, dwells in Him.
And we know by the Spirit in us, that He lives within us.
—I *John* 3:24

When the righteous are in authority, the people rejoice;
but when the wicked rule, the people mourn.
—*Proverbs* 29:2

—*Also see Conscience*

RISK

Behold the turtle. He makes progress
only when he sticks his neck out.
—*James Bryant Conant*

Why not go out on a limb?
After all, that's where the fruit is.
—*Frank Scully*

No one has ever had security. When you leave your house you do not know what will happen on the other side of the door. Anything is possible. But we do not stay at home on that account.
—*Eleanor Roosevelt*

There are two times in a man's life when he should not speculate: when he can afford it, and when he can't.
—*Mark Twain*

—*Also see Caution , Chance, Fear, Luck, & Safety*

SACRIFICE

It is not what we take up, but what we give up, that makes us rich.
—*Henry Ward Beecher*

Greater love hath no man than this: that he lay down his life for his friends.
—*John 15:13*

—*Also see Generosity*

SAFETY

In skating over thin ice, our safety is in our speed.
—*Ralph Waldo Emerson*

Freedom of speech is the greatest safety, because if a man is a fool, the best thing to do is to encourage him to advertise the fact by speaking.
—*Woodrow Wilson*

A warning is like an alarm clock. If you don't pay heed to its ringing, some day it will go off and you won't hear it.

—*Also see Caution, Chance, Fear, & Risk*

SALVATION

No one is so good that he can save himself, and no one is so bad that God cannot save him.

For God so loved the world, that He gave his one and only son, that whosoever believes in Him shall not perish but have eternal life.
—*John 3:16*

For God did not send His Son into the world to
condemn the world, but to save the world through Him.
—*John* 3:17

Whoever believes in Him is not condemned, but
whoever does not believe stands condemned already.
—*John* 3:18

For by Grace you are saved through faith;
and that not of yourselves. It is the gift of God.
Not of works, lest any man should boast.
—*Ephesians* 2:8-9

—*Also see Belief, Faith, Philosophy, & Religion*

SELFISHNESS

Selfishness is the greatest curse of the human race.
—*Gladstone*

What you do for yourself dies with you;
what you do for others is immortal.

The person who lives only for himself finally reaps
nothing but unhappiness. Selfishness corrodes.
Unselfishness ennobles and satisfies. Don't put off the
joy derivable from doing helpful, kindly things for others.
—B.C. *Forbes*

He that findeth his life shall lose it;
and he that loses his life for my sake shall find it.
—*Matthew* 10:39

Real unselfishness consists of
sharing the interests of others.
—*George Santayana*

—*Also see* Conceit & Pride

SILENCE

It is better to remain silent, than to speak the
truth ill-humoredly, and so spoil an excellent
dish by covering it with a bad sauce.
—*St. Thomas de Sales*

Luxury, today, is solitude and silence.
—*Paul-Henri Spaak*

Silence is golden.

—*Also see* Conversation & Speech

Sin

Although it is often couched in
more acceptable terms, sin is still sin.

Sin has many tools,
but a lie is the handle that fits them all.
—Oliver Wendell Holmes

Sin is not hurtful because it is forbidden,
but it is forbidden because it is hurtful.
—Benjamin Franklin

Sin makes its own hell, and goodness its own heaven.
—Mary Baker Eddy

For him who ***knows*** to do good,
and ***doesn't*** do it, it is sin.
—James 4:17

The greatest freedom, is freedom from sin.

—Also see Devil & Evil

SPEECH

Nature has given us two ears, two eyes,
and but one tongue, so we should see
and hear twice as much as we speak.
—*Socrates*

Always use words that build up,
rather than words that tear down.

Speak little. Do much.
—*Benjamin Franklin*

Blessed is the man who has nothing to say,
and abstains from revealing it.
—*George Eliot*

A shut mouth gathers no foot.

Whoever said "Know thyself", should have added
"But don't tell anyone".

Don't be ashamed to say what you
are not ashamed to think.
—*Michel de Montaigne*

The heart of a fool is in his mouth,
but the mouth of a wise man is in his heart.
—*Benjamin Franklin*

The ability to speak effectively is an
acquirement rather than a gift.
—*William Jennings Bryant*

Words are like sunbeams; the more they are
concentrated, the deeper they burn.
—*Robert Southey*

Say not all thou knowest,
but believe all that thou sayest.

Speech is a mirror of the soul; as a man speaks, so is he.
—*Publius Syrus*

When one speaks too much, his words go unheeded.
—*Konrad Adenauer*

The tongue is more to be feared than the sword.
—*Japanese Proverb*

An educated man is one who
knows a lot and says nothing about it.
—*Gracie Fields*

Words are cheap, and deeds are dear.

I don't care how much a man talks,
if he only says it in a few words.
—*Henry Wheeler Shaw.*

The words of the pure are pleasant.
—*Proverbs 15:26b*

When you talk, you are only repeating what you already know—but if you listen, you may learn something.

Let no corrupt communication proceed out of
your mouth, but that which edifies, that it
may minster grace unto the hearers.
—*Ephesians 4:29*

To speak ill of others is a dishonest way of praising ourselves; let us be above such transparent egotism.
—*Will Durant*

He that hath knowledge spareth his words.
—*Proverbs 17:27a*

While thou livest, keep a good tongue in thy head.
—*Shakespeare*

A soft answer turns away wrath;
but grievous words stir up anger.
—*Proverbs 15:1*

We all prefer the ready hand to the ready tongue.

Shun profane and vain babblings,
for they will increase unto more ungodliness.
—*II Timothy 2:16*

If A equals success, the the formula is A =X+Y+Z. X is work, Y is play. And Z is keep your mouth shut.
—*Albert Einstein*

If you don't hold your tongue,
you may have to eat your words.

It is terrible to speak well—but be wrong.
—*Sophocles*

He who guards his mouth preserves his life,
but he who opens wide his lips shall have destruction.
—*Proverbs 13:3*

It is a good policy to leave a few things unsaid.
—*Elbert Hubbard*

Preach Christ, and—if you must—use words.
—*St. Francis of Assissi*

—*Also see Conversation & Gossip*

SPIRIT

The spirit of man is more important than
mere physical strength, and the spiritual
fibre of a nation than its wealth.
—*Dwight D. Eisenhower*

When the spirit of truth comes,
He will guide you into all truth.
—*John* 16:13*a*

The fruit of the spirit is love, joy, peace, patience,
goodness, faithfullness, gentleness, and
self-control. No law prohibits these practices.
—*Galations* 5:22,23

Live by the spirit, and you will not
gratify the desires of the sinful nature.
—*Galations* 5:16

The one who sows to please his sinful nature
will reap destruction; but the one who sows
to please the spirit will reap eternal life.
—*Galations* 6:8

What good will it be for a man if he gains the
whole world but forfeits his soul ? Or what
can a man give in exchange for his soul ?
—*Matthew* 16:26

—*Also see* Belief & Religion

SPORTS

Sports have become the opiate of the American people.

—*Russell Baker*

Dwell not too much upon sports; for they just refresh a man that is weary, as they weary a man who is refreshed.

—*Thomas Fuller*

Sports may develop Characters, not character.

—*Anonymous*

—*Also see Leisure & Idleness*

STRENGTH

It may not be that the race is always to the swift, nor the battle to the strong—but that's the way to bet.

—*Damon Runyon*

Strong men can always afford to be gentle. Only the weak are intent on "giving as good as they get".

—*Elbert Hubbard*

Our strength often increases in proportion to the obstacles imposed on it.

—*Rene Rapin*

What is strength without a double share of wisdom ?
—*Milton*

Strong men are made by opposition;
like kites, they go up against the wind.
—*Henrik Ibsen*

In quietness and in confidence shall be your strength.
—*Isaiah 30:15b*

—*Also see Power*

SUCCESS

Before one can succeed, he must make sure his wish-bone is connected to his backbone.

No one ever climbed the ladder
of success with his hands in his pockets.

You can't get to the top until
you first get off your bottom.

Success is a ladder, not an escalator.

We can't all be top dogs, but each of us can climb a little higher than we already are, and thereby relieve the congestion which exists at the foot of the ladder.

In order to succeed, a man must give
an honest return for the other man's dollar.
—*Edward* H. *Harriman*

The secret to success is to have more
bone in the back and less in the head.

The secret of success is in constancy of purpose.
—*Benjamin Disraeli*

Success is knowing the difference between cornering
people and getting them in your corner.

The successful man is always busy whether he feels like
it or not; any man can work when he feels like it.

Success has ruined many a man.
—*Benjamin Franklin*

Common things, uncommonly done,
pave the way to success.

Money & power are desirable if they can be
obtained without the sacrifice of principle.

The greatest success comes not from money,
power, or fame, but from a happy marriage,
a happy family, and a happy home.
—*Robert Elkington Wood*

He who is resolute & firm will mold the world to himself.
—*Goethe*

If you wish to succeed in life, make perseverance your bosom friend, experience your wise counsellor, caution your elder brother, and hope your gaurdian angel.
—*Addison*

The penalty of success is to be bored by the attentions of people who formerly snubbed you.
—*Mary Lou Wilson*

Success is better when it is harder to achieve.
—*Aristotle*

Everything that was ever accomplished on the face of this earth was achieved with the same equipment that you possess.
—*Herbert Kaufman*

There is but one method of success, and that is hard labor.
—*Sydney Smith*

Thoroughness plus enthusiasm equals success. Try it.
—*Harold A. Holmes*

Industry is the only coin acceptable at the gate of success.

It is only the man who is bigger than his job,
who gets the bigger job.

To succeed in the world,
a man must seem simple, but be wise.
—*Charles D. Montesquieu*

Success comes to those who become success-conscious. Failure comes to those who indifferently allow themselves to become failure-conscious.
—*Napoleon Hill*

It is the old lesson—a worthy purpose, patient energy for its accomplishment, a resoluteness undaunted by difficulties, and then success.
—*William Punshon*

Nothing succeeds like success.
—*Arnold J. Toynbee*

Success in life is a matter not so much of talent or opportunity as of concentration & perseverance.
—*Charles Simmons*

When a man succeeds, he does it in spite of everybody, and not with the assistance of everybody.
—*Edgar Watson Howe*

The secret of success in life is for a man to be ready for his opportunity when it comes.

—*Benjamin Disraeli*

Success depends more upon concentration & perseverance than it does upon talent or opportunity.

Success has killed more men than bullets.

—*Texas Guinan*

Commit to the Lord whatever you do, and your plans will succeed.

—*Proverbs* 16:3 (NIV)

—*Also see* Aim, Ambition, Failure, & Victory

TALENT

Until you try, you don't know what you cannot do.

—*William Feather*

How oft the highest talent lurks in obscurity.

—*Plautus*

No one respects a talent that is concealed.

—*Desiderius Erasmus*

It is a sort of clever stupidity to develop
just one sort of talent—like a carrier pigeon.
—*George* Eliot

The winds and waves are always
on the side of the ablest navigators.
—*Edward Gibbon*

The best evidence of ability is an immense capacity for
hard work and an intense conviction of its necessity.
—*Napoleon* Hill

—*Also see* Ingenuity

TAXES

It shocks a man with his feet on the ground to see a man
with his head in the clouds pay a big income tax.
—*Henry* S. *Haskins*

Behind every successful man stands a wife, a mother,
and the IRS.

The reward of energy, enterprise, and thrift—is taxes.
—*Willaim Feather*

The income tax has made more liars out of
the American people than golf has.
—*Will Rogers*

A taxpayer is a person who has the
government on his payroll.
—*Arnold Glasgow*

The taxes are indeed very heavy, and if those laid by the government were the only ones, we might easily discharge them. But we are taxed ***twice*** as much by our ***idleness***, ***three*** times as much by our ***pride***, and ***four*** times as much by our ***folly***. And from these taxes the commissioners cannot ease or deliver us.
—*Benjamin Franklin*

—*Also see Government*

TEACHING

Your ***example*** means much more than your ***instruction***.

You cannot teach a man anything,
you can only help him to find it within himself.
—*Galileo*

Teaching is not lecturing or telling things. It is devising a sequence of questions which enables folks to become aware of generalizations by themselves.
—*Max Beberman*

Some teachers petrify at forty;
others are at the best in their seventies.
—*G. B. Harrison*

Diligence is the greatest of teachers.
—*Arab Proverb*

Show me thy ways, oh Lord; teach me thy paths.
—*Psalm* 25:4

You cannot, by all the lecturing in the world, enable a man to make a shoe.
—*Samuel Johnson*

I had, out of my sixty teachers, a scant half-dozen who could not have been supplanted by phonographs.
—*Don Herold*

Prosperity is a great teacher, but adversity is a greater one. Possession pampers the mind; privation trains and strengthens it.
—*William Hazlitt*

—*Also see Ignorance, Knowledge, & Learning*

TEMPERANCE

Temperance is the moderating of
one's desires in obedience to reason.
—*Cicero*

Temperance gives vigor and tranquility.
—*William Temple*

Everything that exceeds the bound of
moderation has an unstable foundation.
—*Seneca*

Moderation is the key of lasting enjoyment.
—*Hosea Ballou*

Freedom comes not from satisfying
one's desire, but from controlling it.
—*Epictetus*

—*Also see Desire, & Discipline*

TEMPTATION

You cannot run away from a weakness; you must sometime fight it or perish; and if that is so, why not now, and where you stand ?
—*Robert Louis Stevenson*

If you don't want the fruits of sin,
stay out of the devil's orchard.

People who want to get rich fall into all kinds of temptation and a trap, and into many foolish and harmful desires that plunge men into ruin and destruction.
—I *Timothy* 6:9

When you flee from temptation,
don't leave a forwarding address.

We are not forced into unpleasant activities. We either allow them to happen or encourage them to happen.
—*William Saroyan*

Watch and pray, that ye enter not into temptation; the spirit is indeed willing, but the flesh is weak.
—*Matthew* 26:41

—*Also see* Evil

THANKFULNESS

If you can't be thankful for what you have,
at least be thankful for what you escape.

Don't grumble because roses have thorns,
but rather be thankful that thorns have roses.

Give credit where credit is due: Give thanks to God.
—*Our Daily Bread*

He enjoys much, who is thankful for little;
a grateful mind is both a great and a happy mind.
—*William Secker*

When one is grateful for something too good
for common thanks, writing is less
satisfactory than speech; one does not, at
least, ***hear*** how inadequate the words are.
—*George* Eliot

It is better to say "Thank You" and not mean it,
than to mean it and not say it.

He enjoys much who is thankful for little;
a grateful mind is both a great and a happy mind.
—*William Secker*

In everything give thanks; for this is the will
of God in Christ Jesus concerning you.
—I *Thessalonians* 5:18

—*Also see Blessing*

THOUGHT

Our life is what our thoughts make it.
—*Marcus Aurelius*

Thinking is one of the most difficult of all tasks.
—*Emerson*. (*Which is why few of us do very much of it*)

Thinking is the talking of the soul with itself.
—*Plato*

Thinking is like loving and dying.
Each of us must do it for himself.
—*Josiah Ryan*

Scientists regard it as a major intellectual virtue,
to know what to ***not*** think about.
—C.P *Snow*

The actions of men are the best
interpreters of their thoughts.
—*Locke*

Garner up pleasant thoughts in your mind,
for pleasant thoughts make pleasant lives.
—*John Wilkins*

He that will not command his thoughts
will soon lose command of his actions.
—*Thomas Wilson*

He who considers too much will perform too little.
—*Johann Schiller*

The longer one concentrates on the same train of
thought, the greater the reward for his labor.
—*Sir William Hamilton*

When thought is too weak to be simply expressed,
it's clear proof that it should be rejected.
—*Vanvenargues*

Creative thinking improves as we relate new facts
to the old, and all facts to each other.
—*John Dewey*

Some people study all their life, and at their death they
have learned everything except to ***think***.
—*Francois Domergue*

The man who cannot ***think*** is not an educated man,
however many college degrees he may have acquired.
—*Henry Ford*

The rich are too indolent, the poor too weak,
to support the unbearable fatigue of thinking.
—*William Cowper*

Don't worry too much about what people think,
because they seldom do.

We don't all think alike, but we should all at least ***think***.

If you can get in the last thought,
you needn't worry about getting in the last word.

The thoughts of the wicked are an
abomination to the Lord.
—*Proverbs 15:26a*

—*Also see Ideas & Minds*

TIME

The best way to kill time is to ***work*** it to death.
—*Henry Ford*

Money can be replaced, but time is gone forever.

Lose no time; be always employed in something
useful; cut off all unnecessary actions.
—*Benjamin Franklin*

There are no fragments so precious as those of time, and none are so heedlessly lost by people who cannot make a moment, and yet can waste years.

—*Robert Montgomery*

Time is like money: The less we have to spare, the further we make it go.

—*Henry Wheeler Shaw*

Waste of time is the most extravagant of all expense.

—*Thoephrastus*

Know the true value of time; snatch, seize, and enjoy every moment of it. No idleness. No laziness. No procrastination.

—*Lord Chesterfield*

Time is your only asset. Each moment is a golden treasure, and the way you spend it shapes your life.

Yesterday is dead—forget it. Tomorrow does not exist—don't worry. Today is here—use it!

One today is worth two tomorrows.
Have you something to do tomorrow? Do it today.

—*Benjamin Franklin*

If a man has no time, or only a short time for
seeing people, you can be fairly sure that he
is neither very important or very busy.
—*John Spencer Churchill*

Seize the day. Put no trust in tomorrow.
—*Horace*

This time, like all times, is a good one—
if we just know what to do with it.
—*Ralph Waldo Emerson*

Ordinary people merely ***think*** how to
use their time; a man of intellect actually ***uses*** it.
—*Schopenhauer*

Many take no care of their money till they come to the
end of it, and others do the same with their time.
—*Goethe*

Time is powerless against truth.
—T.H.*Huxley*

The man who wastes today lamenting yesterday
will waste tomorrow lamenting today.
—*Philip* M. *Raskin*

You may delay, but time will not.
—*Benjamin Franklin*

Yesterday is history. Tomorrow is mystery. Today is a gift.
That's why they call it the "present". (Use it wisely !!)

Do not squander time, for that is the stuff life is made of
—*Benjamin Franklin*

When a man at the end of the road casts up
his accounts, he finds that, at best, he has used
only half his life, for good or bad purposes, The
other half was lost inadvertently, like money
dropped through a hole in the pocket.
—*Alfred Polgar*

.Lost time is never found again.
—*Benjamin Franklin*

Time is one's best friend,
teaching best of all the wisdom of silence.
—*A. Bronson Alcott*

—*Also see Economy & Efficiency*

TOLERANCE

Those who cry for tolerance are
usually the most ***in***tolerant of all.

The equal toleration of all religions
is the same thing as atheism.
—*Pope Leo* VIII

Tolerance is most readily achieved
by those who have no convictions.
—*Alexander Chase*

Tolerance is composed of nine parts
of apathy and one part of brotherly love.
—F.M.*Colby*

No human trait deserves less tolerance,
and gets less, than intolerance.
—*Giacamo Leopardi*

Should we tolerate rape, robbery, and murder?
The question is, "Tolerance of ***what***?"

—*Also see* Evil

TRAVEL

The journey of a thousand miles
starts with a single step.
—*Chinese Proverb*

The world is a book, and he who stays at
home reads only one page.
—M..K. *Frelinghuysen*

They change their clime, but not their mind,
who rush across the sea.
—*Horace*

All too often, travel, instead of broadening the mind,
merely lenghtens the conversation.
—*Elizabeth Drew*

—*Also see* World

TRUST

To be trusted is a greater compliment than to be loved..
—*George MacDonald*

Trust everybody—but cut the cards.
—*Peter Finley Dunne*

Trust in God, but keep your powder dry.
—*Cromwell*

Confidence cannot be produced by compulsion.
Men cannot be forced to trust.
—*Daniel Webster*

Trust men and they will be true to you. Trust them greatly and they will show themselves great.
—*Ralph Waldo Emerson*

Trust that man in nothing who has not conscience in everything.
—*Laurence Sterne*

Trust not him that hath once broken faith.
—*Shakespeare*

It is better to trust in the Lord than to trust in man.
—*Psalm* 118:8 (*the very center verse of the entire Bible*)

When you have found out the prevailing passion of any man, remember never to trust him where that passion is concerned.
—*Lord Chesterfield*

Trust in the Lord with all thine heart, and lean not upon thine own understanding.
—*Proverbs* 3:5

Whoever trusts the Lord is happy.
—*Proverbs* 16:20b

—*Also see* Integrity

TRUTH

Some say there is no such thing as an absolute truth.
But that is absurd, because if it were so,
then that statement ***itself*** would be an absolute truth!!

No such thing as an absolute truth??
Does the earth rotate around the sun?

Truth is the only commodity that does not comply
with the Law of Supply and Demand:
The supply is always greater than the demand.

Truth is what stands the test of experience.
—*Albert Einstein*

To know what is false, you must study the truth.

Truth exists, but lies must be invented.
—*George Braque*

Truth is more of a stranger than fiction.
—*Mark Twain*

The man who finds the truth lights a torch.
—*Robert G. Ingersoll*

Live the truth instead of professing it.
—*Elbert Hubbard*

If you are out to describe truth,
leave elegance to the tailor.
—*Albert Einstein*

It is heaven upon earth to have a man's mind
move in charity, rest in Providence, and turn
upon the poles of truth.
—*Francis Bacon*

Style will find readers and shape convictions,
while mere truth gathers dust on the shelf.
—*James Russell Lowell*

For the time will come when they will not endure
sound doctrine; but after their own lusts shall they
heap to themselves teachers, having itching ears;
and they shall turn away their ears from the truth,
and shall be turned into fables.
—II *Timothy* 4:3,4

Rather than love, money, or fame, give me truth.
—*Henry David Thoreau*

To live in the presence of great truths and eternal laws,
to be led by permanent ideals—that is what keeps a
man patient when the world ignores him, and calm and
unspoiled when the world praises him.
—*Balzac*

At a time of universal deceit,
telling the truth is a revolutionary act.
—*George Orwell*

All truth passes through three stages. First, it
is ridiculed, second it is violently opposed,
and third, it is accepted as self-evident.
—*Schopenauer*

Never be influenced by any consideration but
one: Is it the truth? If so, shoot and let the
splinters fall where they may.
—*Eugene* O'Neill

Truth and telling the truth are about as much alike
as moral philosophy and personal memoirs. Also,
we often tell the truth as though that were the
equivalent of doing something about it.
—*Louis* K*ronenberger*

Reality may be fearful, but is less fearful than evad-
ing it—which makes it even more virulent in the
end. Instead, look steadfastly into its eyes, just as
the trainer dominates wild beasts.
—*Cartlin Thomas*

Half of the truth is often a great lie.
—*Benjamim Franklin*

I am the way, the truth, and the life;
no man cometh to the Father but by me.
—*John* 14:6

It is better to know nothing, than to know what isn't so.
—*Josh Billings*

You shall know the truth,
and the truth shall make you free.
—*John* 8:32 (*The obvious corollary is that if you* ***don't*** *know the truth, you will* ***not*** *be free—but rather a slave to whomever or whatever deceives you.*)

Human beings never welcome the news that something they have long cherished is untrue: They almost always reply to that news by reviling its promulgator.
—H.L.*Mencken*

Never be diverted by what you wish or think would be beneficial if it were true; look only at the facts and the truth that bears them out.
—*Bertrand* Russell

Lying lips are an abomination to the Lord,
but those who deal truthfully are His delight.
—*Proverbs* 12:22

A false witness will not go unpunished,
and he who speaks lies shall perish.
—*Proverbs* 19:9

—*Also see* Honesty & Lies

UNDERSTANDING

With all thy getting, get understanding.
—*Proverbs 4:7b*

It is better to understand a little
than to misunderstand a lot.
—*Anatole France*

If the cultivation of the understanding consists in
one thing more than in another, it is surely in
learning the grounds of one's own opinions.
—*John Stuart Mill*

Trust in the Lord with all your heart,
and lean not upon your own understanding.
—*Proverbs 3:5*

Our dignity is not in what we do, but what we understand. The whole world is doing things.
—*Santayana.*

The only thing more exasperating than someone who can't understand is someone who can—but won't.

What the heart knows today,
the head will understand tomorrow
—*James Stephens*

The great understanding in the world is to understand one's own opinions.

Small minds believe only what they can understand. Great minds try to understand what they already believe. (ALL great discoveries have resulted from the latter)

—*Also see Knowledge, Learning, & Wisdom*

VALUE

We should decide how we can be valuable, rather than how valuable we are.
—*Edgar Z. Friedenberg*

A man's value is determined by the ability he ***uses***—not by the ability he ***possesses***.

Things hard to come by are much esteemed.
—*Latin Proverb*

Everything is worth what its purchaser will pay for it.
—*Publius Syrus*

What is valuable is not new, and what is new is not valuable.
—*Daniel Webster*

Man must be disappointed with the lesser things of life before he can comprehend the full value of the greater.
—*Bulwer*

The man who will use his skill and constructive imagination to see how much he can give for a dollar, instead of how little he can give for a dollar, is bound to succeed.
—*Henry Ford.*

Core values are of ***no*** value,
unless they reflect **God's** values.

—Also see Perspective

The weakest spot in any man is where
he thinks himself to be the wisest.
—*Nathaniel Emmons*

We are never so ridiculous by the qualities we have,
as by those we affect to have.
—*LaRochefoucauld*

The man who thinks he has arrived, is already slipping.
—*William Feather*

Nobody is so irritating as someone with less
intelligence and more sense than we have.
—*Don Herold*

Malice, vanity's greatest weapon of defense,
always strikes after the wound has been inflicted.
—*Louis Kronenberger*

Remove me from my vanity and lies.
—*Proverbs 30:8a*

—*Also see Conceit, Pride, & Selfishness*

VICTORY

Don't try to conquer the world. Try to conquer yourself.

Victories that are cheap are cheap. The
only victories worth having are those
which come as a result of hard fighting.
—*Henry Ward Beecher*

When you finish second, no one remembers your name.
—*Frank McGuire*

Be careful that victories do not
carry the seeds of future defeats.
—*Ralph W. Stockman*

The nerve that never relaxes, the eye that never flinches, the thought that never wanders—these are the masters of victory.
—*Edmund Burke*

The secret of all victory lies in the organization of the non-obvious.
—*Oswald Spengler*

—*Also see* Aim, Ambition. Failure, & Success

VIRTUE

He who is virtuous is wise; and he who is wise is good; and he who is good is happy.
—*Boethius*

The simple virtues of willingness, readiness, alertness, and courtesy will carry a young man farther than mere smartness.
—*Henry P. Davison*

The prudent man does good for himself; the virtuous man does good for others.
—*Voltaire*

Self-respect is the cornerstone of all virtue.
—*John Herschel*

It is the will—and not the gift—that makes the giver.
—Gotthold Lessing

Without virtue, no man can find happiness.
—Benjamin Franklin

Do not wait for extraordinary circumstances
to do good actions; try to use ordinary situations.
—Jean Paul Richter

Search others for their virtues, and thy self for thy vices.
—Benjamin Franklin

I see no virtues where I smell no sweat.
—Francis Quarles

If men would consider not so much wherein they differ,
as wherein they agree, there would be far less of
uncharitableness and angry feeling in the world.
—Joseph Addison

The most exhausting thing in life is in being insincere.
—Anne Morrow Lindbergh

The strength of a man's virtue is
no slight evidence of one's own.
—Montaigne

The highest proof of virtue, is to possess
boundless power without abusing it.
—Lord Macauley

Industry, economy, honesty, and kindness form a
quartet of virtue that will never be improved upon.
—*James Oliver*

Whatever things are true, honorable, just, pure,
lovely, or virtuous, think about those things.
—*Philippians* 4:8 (*paraphrased*)

—*Also see Character, Integrity, & Maturity*

WANT

Whoever shuts his ears to the cry of the poor
will also cry himself and not be heard.
—*Proverbs* 21 :13

Human society is based on want. Life is based on want.
Wild-eyed visionaries may dream of a world without
want, but that is cuckoo-land. It can't be done.
—H.G.*Wells*

He who has pity on the poor lends to the Lord,
Who will pay back what he has given.
—*Proverbs* 19:17

—*Also see Generosity & Poverty*

WAR

We have grasped the mystery of the atom,
but rejected the Sermon on the Mount.
—*Gen. Omar Bradley*

Wars are easy. Peacetime is when the trouble begins.
—*Jean Anouilh*

Sooner or later, every war of trade
becomes a war of blood.
—*Eugene V. Debs*

There are few wars in which one
party is wholly in the wrong.
—*Alfred Duggan*

There never was a good war, or a bad peace.
—*Benjamin Franklin*

War is an invention of the human mind;
the human mind can also invent peace and justice.
—*Norman Cousins*

In war, there is no substitute for victory.
—*Dwight D. Eisenhower*

—*Also see Diplomacy & Peace*

WEALTH

Your wealth lies not in what you ***have***,
but in what you would not ***sell*** at any price.

The greatest wealth is contentment with a little.

The love of wealth makes *bitter* men,
but the love of God makes *better* men.
—W. L. *Hudson*

Folks used to deny themselves luxuries
to have money in the bank. Today, they
go without money to have the luxuries.

That man is richest whose pleasures are the cheapest.
—*David Henry Thoreau*

Few rich men own their property;
their property owns them.
—*Robert G. Ingersoll*

He who has little and wants less,
is richer than he who has much and wants more.
—*Charles C. Colton*

Riches serve a wise man but command a fool.
—*English Proverb*

No amount of money can buy the needs of the soul.

The way to wealth depends chiefly on industry and frugality; that is, waste neither time nor money, but make the best use of both. Without industry and frugality nothing will do; with them, everything.
—*Benjamin Franklin*

Prefer loss to the wealth of dishonest gain;
the former vexes you for a time, but the latter
will bring you remorse forever.
—*Chilo*

The gratification of wealth is not found in mere possession or in lavish expenditure, but in its wise application.
—*Cervantes*

Without a rich heart, wealth is an ugly beggar.

For unto whomsoever much is given, of him shall much be required; and to whom men have committed much, of him will they ask more.
—*Luke* 12:48

A miser grows rich by seeming poor;
an extravagant man grows poor by seeming rich.
—*Shakespeare*

If your riches are yours, why don't you take
them with you to t'other world?
—*Benjamin Franklin*

All men's misfortunes proceed from their aversion
to being alone; hence gambling, extravagance,
dissipation, wine, women, ignorance, slander, envy,
and forgetfulness of what we owe to God.
—*Jean de la Bruyere*

Wealth gotten by vanity shall be diminished;
but he that gathers by labor shall increase.
—*Proverbs* 13:11

Gains without pains, are gains made in vain.

Whosoever trusts in his riches will fall,
but the righteous will thrive like a green leaf.
—*Proverbs* 11:28

It is not a sin to have riches,
but it is a sin to fix our hearts upon them.
—*St. John Baptist de la Salle*

A good name is rather to be chosen than great riches.
—*Proverbs* 22:1*a*

The only way for a rich man to be healthy is by exercise and abstinence—to live as if he were poor.
—*Sir William Temple*

—*Also see Money*

Wisdom

Wisdom is the principle thing; therefore, get wisdom;
—*Proverbs* 4:7*a*

The price of wisdom is above rubies.
—*Job* 28:18

Wisdom is the highest achievement of man.
—*Thomas Carlyle*

A prudent question is one half of wisdom.
—*Bacon*

The New Testament contains all the wisdom of the world.
—*Johannes Ewald, Danish poet*

In order to ***act*** wisely, it is not enough to ***be*** wise.
—*Fedor Dostoevsky*

When wisdom entereth into thine heart, and knowledge
is pleasant unto thy soul, discretion shall preserve thee,
and understanding shall keep thee.
—*Proverbs* 2:10,11

An illiterate wise man is less
dangerous than an educated fool.

The wise man does at once what
the foolish man does finally.
—*Gracian*

A man's wisdom is his best friend; folly his worst enemy.
—*William Temple*

The wise man sees in the misfortunes
of others what he should avoid.
—*Publius Syrus*

Search men's governing principles, and consider the
wise, what they shun and what they cleave to.
—*Marcus Aurelius*

Happy is the man that findeth wisdom,
and the man that getteth understanding.
—*Proverbs* 3:13

Much wisdom often goes with fewer words.
—*Sophocles*

As a solid rock is not shaken by a strong gale, so wise persons remain unaffected by praise or censure.
—*Buddha*

He who walks with wise men will be wise,
but the companion of fools will be destroyed.
—*Proverbs* 13:20

Adversity makes a man wise, not rich.
—*John Ray*

Knowledge dwells in the heads replete with thoughts of other men; wisdom in minds attentive to their own.
—*William Cowper*

Wisdom comes by disillusionment.
—*George Santayana*

Speed is good when wisdom leads the way.
—*Edward* R. Murrow

The wise man is satisfied to be right;
the fool must prove others wrong.
—*Chinese Proverb*

Think twice before you speak or act,
and you will speak or act the more wisely for it.

Not by years but by disposition is wisdom acquired.
—*Plautus*

Few people have sufficient wisdom to prefer censure—which is useful—to praise, which deceives them.
—*La Rochefoucald*

Only madmen and fools are pleased with themselves; no wise man is good enough for his own satisfaction.
—*Benjamin Whichcote*

Men who know themselves are no longer fools; they stand at the door of wisdom.
—*Havelock Ellis*

Wisdom is a slow defense against trouble, but at least a sure one.
—*Oliver Goldsmith*

The growth of wisdom may be gauged accurately by the decline of ill temper.
—*Friedrich Nietzsche*

Circumstances are the rulers of the weak; but they are the instruments of the wise.
—*Samuel Lover*

How much better it is to get wisdom than gold, and to get understanding rather than silver.
—*Proverbs* 16:16

The wisdom of the world is foolishness with God.
—I *Corinthians* 3:19

The fool wonders; the wise man asks.
—*Disraeli*

A wise man is strong.
Yes, a man of knowledge increases strength.
—*Proverbs* 24:5

—*Also see Advice, Challenge, Difficulties, & Judgement*

WOMAN

A sufficient measure of civilization
is the influence of good women.
—*Ralph Waldo Emerson*

What a man looks for in a woman is something
like a good piano minus the loud pedal.
What he looks for is tone, modulation, essential
precision, music that is well composed, soft, and lovely.
—*George Jean Nathan*

To know the right woman is a liberal education.
—*Elbert Hubbard*

A virtuous woman is a crown to her husband; but she
that maketh ashamed is as rottenness to his bones.
—*Proverbs* 12:4

Plain women know more about
men than beautiful ones do.
—Katharime Hepburn

Who can find a virtuous wife?
For her worth is far above rubies.
—Proverbs 31:10

—Also see Marriage

WORLD

There are two worlds: the world that we can
measure with line and rule, and the world that we
feel with our hearts and imagination.
—Leigh Hunt

Do not love the world or anything in the world.
If anyone loves the world, the Father is not in him.
—I John 2:15

A baby is God's opinion that the world should go on.
—Carl Sandburg, Poet

—Also see Travel

Worry

Worry kills, but not work.

The reason why worry kills more people than work,
is that more people worry than work.
—*Robert Frost*

Worry is more exhausting than work.
Work hard and you'll have no time to worry.

—*Frank* S. *Bartlett*

Worry never robs tomorrow of its sorrows,
but only saps today of its strength.
—A.J.*Cronin*

Worry ends where faith begins.

Small worries are worst when we are idle and are often
dispersed by motion like a flock of gnats.
—*Charles Horton Cooley*

If you do the best and the most you can today,
don't worry about tomorrow.
—B.C.*Forbes*

The mere *apprehension* of a coming evil has put many into a situation of the utmost danger.
—*Lucan*

Worry is a burden that God never meant for us to bear.

Epilogue

While collecting these adages, quotes, maxims, proverbs, aphorisms, and epigrams whenever I encountered them over the years, I believe I always also recorded the authors, if they were shown. It is at least possible, however, that I inadvertently omitted the source as I wrote them down—simply because it is only within the last few years that I ever considered doing anything with them beyond using them for my own edification and utterance at appropriate moments. So if a source which is known to others is omitted, I apologize. While the authors of those quotes may thus be denied proper credit, we can all still benefit from their wisdom.

In a few cases, I have added a parenthetical remark to complete the thought. In other cases, I have intentionally shortened a quote for the sake of brevity, or re-phrased the original mid-Victorian language to more modern English for clarity. In **NO** case, however, have I changed the context of any of them.

In several cases I have italicized, underlined, or used bold type for emphasis. Where I have both underlined ***and*** used bold type, I recommend the reader not only read it twice, but also ***reflect on its full implications!!!***

In all thy ways acknowledge Him
and He *shall direct thy paths.*

—*Proverbs* 3:16

Alternate Word Index

Abomination . . . . See Evil & Hate
Achievement . . . . See Accomplishment
Act . . . . See Deed or Action
Aid . . . . See Help & Generosity
Benevolence . . . . See Generosity
Bias . . . . See Prejudice
Charity . . . . See Generosity
Choice . . . . See Discretion, Judgement, & Perspective
Coincidence . . . . See Chance & Luck
Commerce . . . . See Business
Conduct . . . . See Behavior
Conflict . . . . See Argument
Conformity . . . . See Perspective
Covetousness . . . . See Desire & Contentment
Custom . . . . See Habit
Deceit . . . . See Lies
Defeat . . . . See Failure
Delight . . . . See Happiness
Demon . . . . See Devil
Direction . . . . See Aim, Purpose, & Motives
Disagreement . . . . See Argument
Discrimination . . . . See Judgement, Prejudice & Perspective
Disgust . . . . See Contempt & Hate

Egotism . . . . . . See Pride & Vanity
Empathy . . . . . . See Kindness
Endurance . . . . . . See Patience & Perseverance
Envy . . . . . . See Desire, Jealousy, & Want
Fairness . . . . . . See Justice
Falsehood . . . . . . See Lies & Truth
Foe . . . . . . See Enemies
Folly . . . . . . See Fools
Freedom . . . . . . See Liberty
Frugality . . . . . . See Economy
Giving . . . . . . See Generosity
Gladness . . . . . . See Happiness
Goals . . . . . . See Aim, Motives & Purpose
Holiness . . . . . . See Righteousness & Conscience
Initiative . . . . . See Accomplishment, Ambition & Perseverance
Insight . . . . . . See Discretion & Perspective
Instruction . . . . . . See Knowledge, Learning, & Teaching
Intelligence . . . . . . See Ingenuity, Minds, & Talent
Intention . . . . . . See Aim & Motives
Joy . . . . . . See Happiness and Contentment
Logic . . . . . . See Common Sense & Reason
Morality . . . . . . See Conscience & RIghteousness
Negotiation . . . . . . See Diplomacy
Notions . . . . . . See Ideas
Obligation . . . . . . See Debt or Duty
Occupation . . . . . . See Business
Optimism . . . . . . See Perspective
Order . . . . . . See Discipline
Parents . . . . . . See Children or Family
Pessimism . . . . . . See Perspective

Piety . . . . . See Righteousness & Conscience
Politeness . . . . . See Courtesy
Problems . . . . . See Difficulties
Procrastination . . . . . See Time
Prosperity . . . . . See Blessing
Quality. . . . . . See Excellence
Questions. . . . . . See Curiosity, Ideas, Minds, & Thought
Reading. . . . . . See Books
Resentment . . . . . See Hate
Restraint . . . . . See Discipline
Satan . . . . . See Evil & Devil
Satisfaction . . . . . See Contentment
Security . . . . . See Liberty, Opportunity, Risk, & Safety
Skill. . . . . . See Ingenuity & Talent
Slander . . . . . See Speech, Gossip, and Lies
Stupidity. . . . . . See Fools
Sympathy . . . . . See Compassion
Tact . . . . . See Diplomacy
Talking. . . . . . See Speech
Thrift . . . . . See Economy & Efficiency
Trade. . . . . . See Business
Training . . . . . See Discipline & Teaching
Trials . . . . . See Difficulties
Trouble . . . . . See Difficulties
Tyrant . . . . . See Dictators & Government
Uncertainty . . . . . See Certainty & Doubt
Warning . . . . . See Caution
Willingness . . . . . See Attitude, Enthusiasm & Cooperation
Wish . . . . . See Desire or Want
Work. . . . . . See Industry

Postscript

*I asked that "*Little Gems*" be published without my name on the cover, to help the reader focus on the author's God, rather than on God's author. After all, it was God who planted all these thoughts in the minds of all those people, it was God who caused them to be both uttered and then recorded for posterity, it was God who caused me to collect them over many years, and it was God who led me to a Publisher who was willing to print them in book form.*

But the Publisher, my very sweet wife, and two trusted friends won the argument. Nevertheless, ALL *the credit belongs to God, and I merely thank* Him *for letting me be involved in making it happen.*

—J.D. Kroft